Secrets
of
Success

KEN EDDY

TAG Publishing, LLC
2030 S. Milam
Amarillo, TX 79109
www.TAGPublishers.com
Office (806) 373-0114
Fax (806) 373-4004
info@TAGPublishers.com

ISBN: 978-1-59930-417-5

First Edition

Quantity discounts are available on bulk orders.
Contact info@TAGPublishers.com for more information.

Secrets
of
Success

10 Reasons why 10% of Realtors
Control 90% of the Business

KEN EDDY

This book is dedicated to my many friends through-out the Real Estate world. Thank you for sharing your experiences, insights and inspiration year after year. We are all in this together and I hope that my thoughts, stories and advice within these pages will help all of you obtain your goals and enjoy the journey.

A special thanks to Cal and Vicki Kellett, Glenn Herring, John Humphreys and Constance Slippy!

Secrets of Success

Contents

Foreword 9

Introduction 11

Preview of the Ten Secrets of Success 27

Secret #1: Know Enough to Know that you Don't Know! 35

Secret #2: Ask that Right Question of the Right Person at the
      Right Time! 45

Secret #3: Adapt and Change with the Times! 53

Secret #4: Take Care of Everything Inside your Four Walls! 61

Secret #5: Use your Strengths! 69

Secret # 6: Personal and Professional Development 83

Secret #7: Industry Knowledge! 117

Secret #8: Build your Network! 125

Secret #9: Have a Written Business Plan! 139

Secret #10: Follow a Schedule! 153

Success and Your Pot of Gold 163

Secrets of Success

Foreword

I have known and worked with Ken for more than twelve years as he fine-tuned every detail of his *Secrets to Success*. Not only did I gain a greater understanding of my own business, but I also discovered what persistence and the simple implementation of these tools can do for any business. As I watched Ken create his Real Estate Training/Seminar Company while still operating and growing a top producing real estate team, I knew the information he was sharing with other Realtors wasn't just theory, it was fact that he lived every single day.

One of the key questions Ken asks Realtors is: *Have you ever wondered why 10% of Real Estate Agents control 90% of sales transactions and consequently the same percentage of commissions?* Ken suggests that if you haven't asked yourself this question as a real estate professional, then you're definitely not in the 10% and the *Secrets of Success* is a must-read for you.

As a Realtor, you literally own and operate your own business. You owe it to yourself to know everything there is to know about that business and the industry in which you work. This book lays out the fundamentals of owning, operating, and advancing your real estate business and includes everything from developing your personal communication and networking skills to creating an annual business plan. All of this information is set out in understandable, easy-to-implement terms.

If you're questioning your networking skills, struggling with self-esteem, or even wondering how you'll ever become successful in such a competitive industry, *Secrets of Success* will provide the answers for these questions and more, while giving you the tools to advance your business exponentially.

Over the years I have worked all of the concepts in Ken's *Secrets of Success* into my own business with impressive results and I continually re-read this book to remind myself of what I need to do to take my business to the next level. As a Realtor, or for that matter as the owner of any business, *Secrets of Success* should be at the top of your reading list, especially if you're planning on becoming unbeatable in your industry.

Secrets of Success

Ken's inspirational sense of humour, his common sense and practical business policies will prove to be the perfect stepping stones to make your business a winner.

Cal Kellett

Author/Entrepreneur/Entertainer/Business Owner/Friend

Introduction

We humans love to discover secrets - especially good secrets. We like ones that surprise, shock, enlighten, and inspire us with all that they reveal. Is it because they offer us a type of forbidden fruit? Possibly a tidbit of elusive information that only a select few are privy to? Perhaps. But whatever it may be, it is up to us to take advantage of these newfound secrets, since these secrets may help you realize things that you may never have otherwise come across and, quite possibly, change your direction and, in turn, your life.

I have achieved tremendous success as a Realtor, not because I'm the smartest guy in the room, but because I've watched, listened, and sometimes discovered the hard way, that there are certain secrets of success that can make or break your business. I'm frequently asked the same questions repeatedly by other Realtors: "How did you do it? What am I doing wrong? How do I achieve the kind of long-term success that will secure my future?"

The truth is that it's not easy, but it's also not nearly as hard as so many people assume it to be. There are shortcuts to success and most of those have to do with how you think and approach your business. I wrote this book so I could share some of the most important secrets that I've discovered and these will form the foundation of a successful real estate sales business for those people who really want to succeed.

"Realization" is a word that will pop into your mind as you discover how significant each of these secrets are and how they can, if understood and applied correctly, have a profound effect on your business, allowing you to turn a struggling career into a successful and rewarding one.

Some of these realizations may make sense to you gradually, while others will hit you like an epiphany, causing you to ask yourself why you had not -what's the word?-"Realized" that before!

Secrets of Success

Though some of these secrets may seem obvious, or may even be something you have heard in another way before, unless you really grasp each idea fully, you will still struggle to achieve your goals.

Not only will these ideas change your outlook on the future of your business, but they will also dictate the outcome of your day-to-day performance, boosting you to greater heights than you can imagine right now.

In this book, I will reveal my Ten Success Secrets designed to help make you money and save time - all the while enjoying your business and work life.

But before we dive into these secrets, you need to ask yourself a few questions in order to fully understand what is really happening out there in the real estate sales world.

Questions like:

- Why is it that 10% of the Realtors control 90 percent of the sales transactions and, of course, earn 90 percent of the commissions?
- Why is it that this same small group of Realtors always seems to have a steady stream of leads, month after month, year after year and run a healthy, profitable business, - no matter how the economy is performing?
- Why is it that these top Realtors always appear to be in a good mood, with that glass half full type of attitude that tends to annoy everyone else who is struggling?
- You consider yourself a hard worker, you do a great job for your clients and you always put their interests first, right? So why is it, like the majority of Realtors, you often find yourself struggling year after year, always feeling like you're trapped behind the eight ball and never getting ahead?

Years ago, I found myself wondering the very same things during the first few years of my career. Believe it or not, I wasn't always successful and I had to deal with a steep learning curve. I started in real estate in the summer of 1988. My city (Calgary, the oil capital of Canada) was just starting to recover from a devastating recession that saw housing prices drop 40% in just twelve months.

At that time, the economy and the real estate market were on the road to recovery, but at a snail's pace. We needed confidence in the real estate market; we needed buyers and we needed lower interest rates to spur the economy on since, at the time, the interest rates were still north of 15%.

I was truly amazed that, even in this market, there was a group of Realtors, albeit a small group, doing very well.

I would watch with envy as they continued to rack up sale after sale when I could scarcely find a listing to work with, let alone a serious buyer.

Why, I asked, do the few achieve so much while the bulk of us struggle just to survive in the industry?

The truth of the matter is that there is no "Middle Class" in real estate sales. It's either feast or famine. Realtors find themselves either in the top 10% and enjoying the success and the fruits of their labor or struggling in the bottom 90%, perhaps living from one commission cheque to another!

What were these top Realtors doing that I was not doing? While it was easy to assume they had some special edge, the truth is that they didn't. They were just like me - except they had already discovered the same secrets I will share with you and they applied them to their business.

Most Realtors struggle their entire career without even scratching the surface of understanding what it takes to be part of the top 10%. They get frustrated, angry, and blame everyone else but themselves. I did this too at first. But this lack of understanding and knowledge are the main reasons why one third of Realtors quit every year or hang their license at a "part time" agency just waiting and praying for the business to just come walking through the door. Or, they sit back and hope that their friends, relatives, and just dumb luck will give them a chance to make a sale.

There are just over one hundred thousand licensed Realtors in Canada and approximately one million in the United States. In both countries, the average Realtor sold only three houses last year and we all know that when you calculate this average, there are a lot more Realtors selling below the average then above. As a matter of fact, throughout the United States in 2011, 35% of real estate agents sold absolutely nothing. Wow! How do they survive? Truthfully, they don't! They either quit or find other means of additional income to help subsidize and make ends meet.

Secrets of Success

By 1993, after five years in the trenches, I was prepared to pack it in. Despite my best efforts, I was just not quite getting the plane off the ground. I had just taken custody of my two children, ages 15 and 13 at the time, my bills were piling up, and the prospects of much-needed listings and buyers were looking mighty slim at best.

I had pretty much reached the end of the line and had actually told my broker (owner of the office) that I was leaving and had found another career to pursue. Then, at the last possible moment, the new career evaporated. I suddenly not only had nothing, I had nowhere to go. I realized then that I could not rely on anyone else; I had to take 100% control of my future for the simple fact that no one else really cared remotely as much as I did whether I succeeded or not.

Now as upsetting as the situation was at the time, it turned out to be the best thing that could have happened to me. Of course, you are thinking that everyone who succeeds in overcoming a huge challenge always says that, but the truth of the matter is that it made me re-focus and try even harder than I had before - which is exactly what I needed to do. I realized that I had no choice; I had to succeed in real estate sales because absolutely everything depended on it. That very next month, back in 1993, I sold two houses and I have never looked back, growing my business month-by-month, year-by-year, client-by-client. Now, I can proudly say that my team and I average transactions into the double digits each month – but it didn't just happen; it took a lot of effort.

Looking back, I can say that I felt a bit like Alexander the Great, arguably the greatest empire builder the world has known. When he arrived with his Greek troops on the shores of the Western edge of the Persian Empire (modern-day Turkey), they were vastly outnumbered. He knew it would be very easy for a reasonable person to look at the situation and decide immediately on retreat. That is how I felt at the low point of my real estate career - that retreat was the obvious choice.

But Alexander the Great would not accept defeat and he understood the idea that a man with no choice will fight to the death. So he ordered all of his army's boats burned. This meant they could not retreat and that their very lives depended on victory. Rumour has it that Alexander told his troops "We go home in Persian ships or we die".

This was exactly my situation. I had thought that I was going to be able to escape to another job, but when it evaporated, I had no choice but to recommit fully to real estate sales.

When you commit to a goal with all your energy and focus, and with no means of retreat, then doors and opportunities open up and appear for you. That was the situation I was in.

I knew there was no turning back; I was 100% committed to being successful in real estate sales. Doors did open up and opportunities appeared for me, but only with a lot of hard work and determination.

We are all faced with challenges in our businesses and lives. Some are big and some are small. At the end of the day, it is how you handle the challenges that will make the difference between success and failure and the easiest road rarely produces the best results.

Over the past few years, the United States has been facing a huge challenge in its real estate market.

They are struggling through a devastating housing and financial crisis that still does not seem to have found the bottom. Every time I attend an international real estate convention, I discover through speakers and my fellow Realtors that in vast sections of the market, the United States still has a ways to go before they even start to turn the corner. They are saddled with a tremendous amount of excess real estate inventory and troubled by a general lack of confidence - not only in real estate, but also in the overall economy.

Is there light at the end of the tunnel? I would have to say yes, albeit at the expense of a lot of hard working families a high percentage of whom, through no fault of their own, are losing their homes or, at the very least, have lost a huge chunk of their equity.

At the time of this writing, there have been over nine hundred US-based banks go under, but in Canada there have been absolutely none. The conservative lending practices of the Canadian banks have saved the Canadian citizens from following in the footsteps of their American cousins. You could say that Canadians learned a valuable lesson without having to pay a huge price!

Secrets of Success

In a large number of markets throughout the United States, if you are not a Realtor who specializes in foreclosures, distressed properties, or short sales you are starving. The top Realtors in the hardest hit areas have had to re-think and re-tool their business models in order to stay afloat. Now, that is not to say that there are no foreclosures in Canada -because there certainly are. But, not even remotely close to what is happening south of the border.

As we all know, the Canadian and U.S. economies are joined together at the hip; they are each other's largest trading partners. This symbiotic relationship will only get stronger as we move forward with Canada's natural resources and with the U.S. still having the world's largest economy.

For Canadians, when you sleep next to the elephant, you better pay attention to which way he is rolling, so it is best that you sleep with one eye open so you don't get crushed - especially now, since the U.S. seems to be experiencing a bit of a nightmare.

Lessons have been learned, expectations (and maybe even values) have been adjusted, but mark my words - the American economy will come roaring back and the next generation will want and expect more than the current generation.

The new recharged, revised, and re-focused U.S. economy will come steam-rolling down the tracks and, as real estate professionals, we better be prepared to jump aboard for the ride!

Paying attention to international and national events, world economics, and various real estate markets across the country is important for the simple fact that you have to be aware of what is transpiring that may have an affect your local market in a positive or negative way to a certain degree.

However, as important as it is to know these facts and the events that are transpiring, it is more important to know that there is absolutely nothing you can do about them!

Too often Realtors waste their valuable time and energy worrying and fretting about events and markets that they cannot control or which may or may not affect them locally.

Instead, they should focus on the one thing that they can control and that is their own business!

In the pages ahead, you will discover key aspects and characteristics that top Realtors have incorporated into their businesses. These ideas are essential for you to incorporate into your business as well in order to reach your full potential.

You will understand why top Realtors are just that - top Realtors! You will also understand the importance of taking charge of your own education and career. This means not leaving it to others to lead you or simply lying back and hoping business just happens.

More importantly, you will know and believe that you are capable of becoming a top Realtor yourself. Before I get started revealing the ten secrets, I would first like to dispel some myths that many people have about top Realtors.

Everyone has an opinion of just why those top 10% of the Realtors are doing 90% of the business and why they continue to grow, despite the market conditions, with a steady flow of leads and sales month after month and year after year.

Early in my career, I thought that those top Realtors were lucky, that they were probably born into a rich family with endless connections, that they just always happen to be at the right place at the right time, or had simply just lead charmed lives. So how could I possibly compete with them? You may have made (or are making!) some of these same assumptions. Even still, you might assume that it is men who get all the leads - or if you are a man, you might think that it is easier for women to get leads.

If you are making any of these assumptions, I am afraid that you are wrong on all counts. They are all just excuses and myths and none of them are true. You will soon discover that all those excuses you might have been using, and the myths that you have believed over the years, have nothing to do with the tremendous success of top Realtors. The biggest difference between you and them is that top Realtors don't buy into the myths or use excuses!

Secrets of Success

Let's go a little farther and debunk some of the other excuses and myths:

Is it age?

Whether you are 28 or 58, whether you are soaring in the real estate sales business or suffering, with only a few years of experience, your business can start growing rapidly and steadily. Have a look at your office or your company and you will find young Realtors putting up big numbers and young Realtors struggling. That also applies to the Realtors that have been in the game for twenty plus years, for they, too, can struggle or can be extremely successful.

As we all know, success can be defined several different ways - from monetary gain, to family, health, and spiritual well-being to name a few. When I write about success in this book, I am referring to a balance between life and work, combined with a healthy net-profit - not just gross sales.

For example, a friend of mine, Joel, started his real estate career at the ripe old age of 18. One of the very first things he did was to start working with an experienced senior Realtor in his office. His energy and enthusiasm for the business was contagious. Within the first few years he, and his mentor's sales reached new heights. After eight years, he ventured out on his own, taking what he had learned from his terrific mentor and has never looked back growing his business year after year. Joel now has one of the top teams in his office.

Now, let's look at Adrianna, a 47 year old executive that had enough of the corporate world. After having recently sold her house and downsizing into a condo, she was intrigued by the whole sales process. Since the real estate agent she had hired was a friend of hers, she was privy to the inner workings of the transaction and got an inside look at what being a Realtor was like.

Chatting over a few glasses of wine with her real estate agent friend about the possibility of getting into real estate sales, her decision was made. Adrianna made a dramatic change in her life and put the wheels in motion to obtain her real estate license.

Of course, some of her friends thought that she was crazy to leave a solid salary-based job, but by leveraging her past job experience and contacts, and by taking advantage of all the educational tools, advice, and guidance that was available to her, she went on to become one of the top Realtors in her office in a matter of less than five years.

So, no, it is not age!

Is it gender?

If you take the time to examine the top Realtors in your company, or even just in your office, you will see that it is usually 50/50 between male and female agents in the upper level of sales achievement. Just recently, I returned from an international real estate awards conference in Las Vegas where individual agents and teams are honoured with a wide-range of awards including total transactions, gross dollar volume, and lifetime achievement.

When I look at the long list of these top producers, from the likes of Christopher Invidata from Oakville, Ontario to Joyce Tourney from Regina, Saskatchewan, it is easy to see that sales success does not favour either gender. Some clients will prefer to work with a male and others a female, but the majority just want to work with a true professional and don't really have a gender preference. Christopher and Joyce are outstanding Realtors and it is no surprise to me that they achieve such a great success year after year.

So, no, it is not gender!

Is it Ethnic heritage?

Let me dispel this myth by relating to you the story of my friend and fellow agent Tommy Low. Tommy grew up in Winnipeg Manitoba; he is of Chinese heritage and graduated college with a degree in accounting. Tommy then decided, like a lot of young men, to head out on his own. So, he moved to Calgary in the early 1980s.

Back then, Calgary was about as redneck as you could get and Tommy moseyed into town hardly knowing a soul.

He then had the bright idea that he was going get into real estate sales. It turned out to be a very good idea since Tommy became one of the top Realtors in his office.

Now, let's review the facts:

- Tommy is of Chinese heritage.
- He moved to a redneck city where he hardly knew a soul.
- Tommy became one of the top Realtors in his office.
- But here is the real kicker: Tommy stands just four feet two inches tall! That's right - Tommy is a little person.

Tommy's motto is "Big results from the little guy"! Now, if that doesn't dispel a few myths, nothing will. Ten years ago, Tommy had some health issues and decided to retire from real estate sales. After a couple of serious operations, Tommy was confined to a wheelchair, but that did not stop him.

Incredibly, last Fall, Tommy decided to get back into real estate along with his friend Erica, who is relatively new to the industry. A few months later, they are churning out the sales left, right, and centre! So if you think you have some challenges that are holding you back from being successful, maybe it is time to re-think that idea.

Look around and you will discover that top Realtors are from all nationalities and backgrounds.

So, no, it is not ethnic heritage (and obviously not height either)!

Is it family connections?

Growing up in your real estate market-place can possibly have advantages. Perhaps you have a large extended family that you can rely on for business, but even that has its pros and cons. Some family members might never do business with a relative for fear of conflict and others might not look at you as a real professional because they remember back when you were making mud pies at five years old.

Look around and you will discover that over half the top Realtors out there were not born in the market place that they currently do business in and a large percentage of them were not even born in this country.

There is a large cross section of the population that just expects to be successful simply because they were born in North America, but from my observations I have discovered that when someone moves here from a different country, they do not just expect that they will just automatically become successful. They know they have to work for it and are prepared to do so.

So, no, it is not family connections.

Is it because of their good looks?

In today's society, there is a lot of emphasis placed on physical attractiveness, body type and sex appeal. Fortunately, though, it has nothing to do with whether or not you will be successful in real estate sales. As a matter of fact, in a lot of cases it can be a burden.

Some individuals are blessed with extremely good looks (according to fashion magazines), but this can also work against them. For example, a young 27 year old female that looks like she should be walking down the fashion runways in Paris may have a very hard time convincing sellers that she can seriously sell their home. In addition, some wives really do not want Miss Universe hanging around their husband, if you get my drift!

So, no, looks have nothing to do with it (thank goodness)!

Is it because they have an easy life?

I could point you in the direction of Tommy again to dispel this myth, but you will soon realize that a lot of the top Realtors have had major struggles and setbacks in their own lives. They have overcome them, become tougher, and learned how to handle life's challenges. They were forced to adapt and change, prioritize, and persevere. Like the saying goes, "What does not kill you, makes you stronger."

For example, I know a Realtor who is a single mother of three that balances an extremely chaotic home life with her real estate sales career.

She still manages to out-perform her fellow Realtors that have limited outside responsibilities.

I have had the opportunity to not only talk to, but also to interview, top Realtors from across North America.

During these interviews, I am astounded at how many of these top Realtors that seem to have the Midas touch, have also battled cancer, problems with their children, parents, drug and alcohol addiction, or even financial issues from unrelated business ventures. But they still manage to operate their real estate business like they don't have a care in the world and are very successful.

Top Realtors do not let life's trials and tribulations derail them - they adapt and overcome! I know Realtors that work through injuries, sickness, and the worst of what life can throw at them because they know they really do not have a choice. They have to get out there and get to work, dig up the leads, work with the clients, and close the transactions because they are fully aware that nobody else is going to do it for them. Top Realtors are not 'coasters;' they do not sit back and rest on their laurels or expect someone else to carry them along.

They work hard at their careers and reap the benefits because of it.

If you are like me, you probably enjoy reading biographies of some or our world's most successful and famous people. I am always amazed to discover the many hardships and challenges that these people have had to overcome through-out their lives. I find that very inspirational and motivational. If I can recommend one book that would inspire you, it would be A Long Walk to Freedom, an autobiography of Nelson Mandela. Now there is a gentleman that had to overcome and persevere through years of hardship and struggle, the likes of which most of us could never fathom.

So, no, it is not that they have had an easy life!

Is it because they are just lucky?

You might think that luck would be a buyer or seller walking into your office when you just happen to be on floor duty and want to buy or sell a million dollar house. Well, yes, I guess you could call that luck but is that really going to happen 100 times per year? I do not think so! There is a saying that "you have to be good to be lucky."

Those that seem to be lucky in their real estate business have often spent literally decades slogging away in the trenches to make it happen. It is much like a professional athlete you hear about suddenly bursting onto the scene and winning every award possible in their sport. It may seem like overnight success, but what you don't see was the many years of day in, day out dedication that developed them into becoming one of the best in the sport.

If I were you, I would concentrate more on being good at your craft versus just relying on lady luck to come walking through the door.

So, no, it is not just luck!

These were just a few of the many excuses and myths that struggling Realtors use day after day to justify their lack of sales and success. Right now, you may be thinking of a few more excuses that you have leaned on in the past or perhaps still do today.

Now is the time to say to yourself, "No more excuses, no more believing in myths. It is time to get real, get up and get selling".

One good thing about real estate sales is that you can start your career over every day!

Most businesses have to sign long term contracts, tie-up valuable assets and invest a substantial amount of capital to get their companies off the ground and keep them going.

Fortunately a real estate sales career does not require the Realtor to invest tens of thousands of dollars, if not more, just to get started. There is no need to break the bank, to buy a warehouse full of inventory, or invest your life's savings into equipment, labour contracts, or even lease your own office space since most brokerages provide that for you. However, like a lot of companies and businesses, there can be a gap between the start-up date and that first pay cheque. But you can, if you run your real estate career like a business, shorten that gap, eliminate future gaps, and be up and running almost immediately.

Realtors have the luxury of being able to make crucial and necessary adjustments quickly and as often as needed. This gives the Realtor the opportunity to change direction, make the appropriate adjustments, and to adapt to the ever-changing market conditions.

Secrets of Success

There may be times that you have to invest more money into your business as well as times where you can cut-back and save some coin.

So often in business it is easy to get caught up in the thrill of expansion and growth. In real estate sales, if your timing is right and the market gets hot while being positioned with a large inventory of homes, sales take off and money rolls in the door like there is no tomorrow. You might then decide it is time to buy that new vehicle, sign a yearlong magazine advertising contract, and hire a new assistant or two. You are going to rock the real estate world; everything you touch turns to 'sold' and the good times look like they will never end.

Well, my friend, remember that saying: "A high tide floats all boats." So, whether you strategically positioned yourself to take advantage of the hot market or the stars just happen to have finally aligned, you cannot forget to pay the bills and take care of the little things that helped get you there.

Because slowly, but surely, bad habits sneak into our lives, expenses get out of control, and bills don't get paid. Even worse - taxes are put off until later (a bad move in any market).

Most people act surprised when the tough times come back to bite them in the butt. Sales suddenly slow down, inventory and expenses start to pile up, debt collectors are phoning you and, yes, even the government comes calling for its pound of flesh.

You cannot ignore the warning signs. You always have to pay attention to the details when you are running your own business - no matter how good things seem at the time.

Your current sales, listings, and the balance of your bank account are your reality. But, understand that real estate runs in cycles. A strong market will always come to an end sooner or later and you have to be prepared to deal with it when it does.

Keep your head up and be aware of what is going on around you so you can make the necessary adjustments when the time comes. If you have the habit of simply ignoring a problem, hoping that it will just go away, and live with a false believe that things will just get better by themselves, think again.

We can evade reality but we cannot evade the consequences of evading reality.

-Ayn Rand

No matter what market you are in, keep your financial house in order, cut costs where you can, and invest the rest wisely. If you are in the real estate sales business for the long haul, you will experience good times and bad times but remember this: *bad times do not ruin a company, good times do!* When things are bad, we are on guard and ever vigilant, but when things become better and money is flowing like water, we over extend and stop paying attention.

Top Realtors always pay attention to their bottom line, cut costs when they have to, and invest when the time is right. They live in today's reality with the knowledge and understanding that the market is always changing, and so must you change.

As I have stated top Realtors are top Realtors for good reasons. They have discovered the *"Secrets of Success"*. They understand the key aspects and characteristics of what it takes to be successful in today's real estate sales world.

They incorporate those truths into their business on a daily, weekly, monthly, and yearly basis.

They do not let the economy of other countries or the market in other regions stop them and they sure do not let the struggles and whining of other Realtors derail them, slow them down, or prevent them from reaching their goals.

As you read the rest of this book, not only will we uncover ten Secrets of Success, you will also understand:

- The importance of taking charge of your own education.
- How to create an effective business plan tailored to your personal strengths.
- How to work with a schedule that can be just like a business partner helping to put your plan in motion.
- You will also believe that you to are capable of becoming a top Realtor

Make today the day you decide to take back control of your future!

Secrets of Success

Preview of the Ten Secrets of Success

Secret #1

Know enough to know that you don't know!

Like most things in life, things are easier said than done. This certainly applies to real estate sales since practically everyone believes that just because they grew up in a house, that they are fully capable of having a successful career selling real estate. After all, how hard can it be?

Realtors are professionals and while selling real estate may look easy, it is very detailed business, concerns large amounts of money, precision, and skill. Additionally, each Realtor is also an entrepreneur and must run his or her own business in addition to selling real estate.

In this chapter, we will discuss the importance of being honest with yourself and understanding that you are not born with the knowledge to do everything well. You must accept this fact and seek the right kind of help and guidance along the way.

Secret #2

Ask the right question of the right person at the right time!

Nothing will grow your career faster than getting great advice from the right sources. You will be faced with many questions and challenges throughout your career. It is imperative to know who to ask, what to ask, and when to ask for help. There is a virtual art form to it - a relative formula you should adopt and follow on how to prepare, approach, and ask the right questions of the right person at the right time. There is no need for you to waste unnecessary time and resources. Trust me, the wheel has already been invented!

Secret #3

Adapt and change with the times!

It has been said that the only constant in life is change and this certainly applies to the real estate sales world.

From how we communicate with our clients and with our colleagues to how we adapt to new rules and regulations, we must strive to be leaders in our field all while staying in tune with our client's expectations. Change is clearly inevitable. You must be aware of the changes that take place within the industry and know what to focus on so you don't needlessly waste time, energy, and money. Change with the times or be left behind.

Secret #4

Take care of everything inside your four walls!

Do you spend more time and energy worrying about things that are totally out of your control instead of focusing on what is in your control? If there is a recession going on, my advice to you is not to participate. Seriously; is the Greece debt crisis really hurting your business or is it the water cooler talk - that negative chatter that generally focuses on what is wrong in the world instead of what is right?

Recognizing what you ultimately have control over and addressing those concerns is the key to having a successful business, no matter the economic environment. Worrying and fretting about situations that have no bearing on your business in the first place will just prevent that success.

Control what you can control and refuse to worry about everything else.

Secret #5

Use your strengths!

You know that it is impossible for one person to be good at everything. This includes you! What is possible is the fact that you can use your strengths to your advantage, practically ignore your weaknesses, and still become extremely successful. Did I just hear a sigh of relief?

Think about what you are really good at. Can you recognize your strengths? By utilizing simple self-analysis exercises, you will be able to recognize and incorporate your strengths into your daily business and life. Changing your focus to work with your strengths will not only help increase your income, but you will enjoy the process a whole lot more.

Secret # 6

Personal and professional development!

Top Realtors are constantly improving on their personal and professional attributes. They understand that it is not possible to install the second floor windows of your house when you have not even poured the foundation. Your personal and professional attributes have to be cemented into your foundation, added to, and improved in order for the remainder of your business to have a firm base upon which to build. Even though you may not be building a house, you still have to start from the ground up when you are building a solid sustainable business and not get ahead of yourself.

There are certain key characteristics, strengths, attitudes, and disciplines that are the building blocks of your business and career.

These include:

- Ensuring that you have support from your family and friends.
- Always maintaining a positive attitude.
- Enhancing your organizational and delegation skills.
- Discipline and Respect.

All of these are just a few of the key areas you must attend to in order to be successful.

We will explore the importance of these personal and professional attributes and you will see the connection between them and your success and the pot of gold at the end of the rainbow. In addition, you will discover which one of your specific building blocks/attributes are solid and need no attention and which ones are cracked, unstable, or just plain missing. You will learn that some of these skills and tasks are better to be delegated for someone else to accomplish while others can be ignored completely, since you may be so strong in other areas that you can live without them.

Secret #7

Industry knowledge!

"Knowledge is something you get after you know everything" (This is a good line to use on your teenage kids!)Knowledge is power. Knowledge of your industry gives you the edge over your competition.

In today's fast paced information age, you have to keep up or get run over. Reading a book, listening to downloads, attending seminars, and asking questions are critical ingredients for your success. There is more information available today than there has ever been in the history of organized real estate sales. Just like opportunity, knowledge does not come knocking; it is your job to go out and get it.

Secret #8

Build your network!

It is certainly true in the real estate sales world that the whole is greater than the sum of its parts! You cannot do it all by yourself and no matter how many advantages and skills you may already have, you will still need help along the way. Your connections, allies, and supporters are part of your team. Together, you will grow and thrive; individually you will die on the vine.

As with a sports team, everyone has a position to play, so you need to gather your players, fill the holes, and work together for everyone's best interest. Like the Three Musketeers, "All for one and one for all" should be your motto.

Secret #9

Have a written business plan!

What is your plan for making money? You must have some idea, don't you? Or are you like the 90% of all Realtors who just wait for whatever comes down the pipe?

Having a written business plan is an essential element on the road to your success that you can't leave out.

A plan allows you to think about exactly where you are going and you must have this in place before you begin the journey. Otherwise, it is much like starting a trip with no map – you may have the best intentions in the world, but no idea where you are going or how to get there!

In this chapter, I will show you how to create a simple but effective business plan that is tailored to your budget, likes and dislikes and that utilizes your strengths.

You will understand which sources produce your current business and where the highest profit lies.

Then you will be able to create a system for tracking and growing your business into the future. Sure, you can sell real estate without a business plan, but you can sell a heck of a lot more with one!

Secret #10

Follow a schedule!

I can hear you now - "I don't need to follow any kind of schedule"! Sorry to have to tell you this but, yes you do. A schedule is your friend because it helps you put your business plan to work and, as your time becomes better organized, it also allows you to take more time off.

If you truly want to be effective every day, week, month, and year you have to follow a schedule. The good news is that, just like the business plan, you can create a schedule that fits your lifestyle - not one that controls your life.

Unlike most other industries, the structure of a real estate sales business is a very tough one to describe, let alone understand where everything fits. So, I have created the figure below to help you see the big picture. Just like the mighty pyramids, constructed of massive blocks of stone placed intricately together layer upon layer, making it so solid that even millenniums of time cannot bring it down, a real estate sales business is built on the same premise.

The key, of course, is to construct your business on a solid foundation. Your foundation may not be made out of blocks of limestone, but out of substances that can be just as strong and vital to the structure as a whole.

These are your personal traits, strengths, characteristics, plans, and schedules.

Recognizing these building blocks and their role in your life/business, plus the importance of fixing the cracked ones or even finding and inserting the missing ones, will become so apparent to you that if you discover a problem with your business structure, you will know that it is imperative that you act quickly to address it - knowing that if you don't, your business could collapse like a house of cards.

Structure of a Real Estate Business

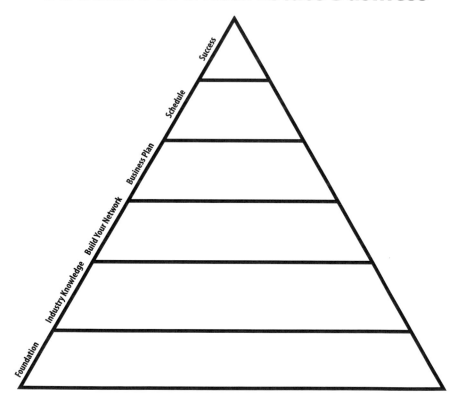

I will be taking you through each level of the pyramid, from the foundation to the pinnacle. As you read through the list of requirements, characteristics, and key aspects of each level, you will see how each secret plays a significant role in the construction of a solid business model. You may think of other points that are not listed, points that will be very important to you and your career. So, once again, just because I have not listed them, does not mean that they are not important.

Secrets #1 through #6 make up the Foundation level of your business. Each of these secrets consists of several building blocks that are all an integral part of your business as a whole. Throughout your career, you have to be vigilant in evaluating and improving your foundation. As your business grows, so will the importance of having an even stronger and more complete foundation.

Secret #1

Know Enough to Know that You Don't Know!

Structure of a Real Estate Business

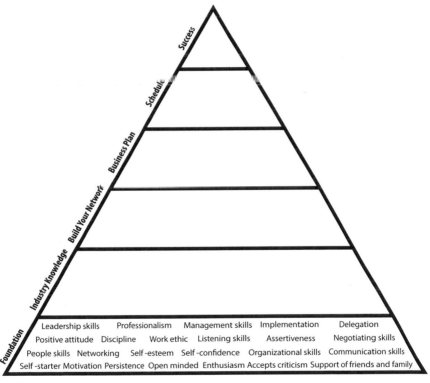

This is where it all starts - having the ability to say to yourself, "I do not know how to do this".

Imagine you are on a plane and the flight attendant leans over, tells you that the pilot and co-pilot have passed out, and then asks you if you can fly a plane.

Secrets of Success

Once you have absorbed the words that she has uttered, you think - "NO, I don't know how to fly a plane; perhaps we should find someone that does".

Now this is a good thing because you have recognized the important fact that you do not know how to fly a plane and have no intention of pretending that you do - for your own sake and of course everyone else's on the plane.

However, with real estate sales, many people mistakenly believe it is easy or simple, so they wrongly assume they can do it. After all, we all grew up in houses, so really, how hard can it be to sell one?

Now think back to a house party you may have attended in the past. Everyone is gathered in the kitchen and there is an acquaintance there - let's call him "Sven". Sven is giving his opinion to everyone who cares to listen on how he would improve the value of the house by changing the decor, having a smaller sofa, different paint colour, and livening up the window coverings. Inevitably someone says, "Sven, you are so good at interior designing, you should be a Realtor. You would be great".

This kind of statement makes me so angry because there is the assumption that someone who is good with paint colours can also understand and negotiate complex contracts, work effectively with buyers and sellers, run their own business, and make a profit. This kind of comment also gives Sven the idea that he can make a quick buck in real estate sales when he probably has no clue what is required.

Now I can tell you that, yes, it is nice to be able to colour coordinate and give staging advice to your clients, but it has virtually nothing to do with being a successful Realtor or being a successful interior designer/stager for that matter.

This is a classic example of how a little bit of knowledge can be a dangerous thing. If Sven or anybody else stakes his or her future on a little bit of interior design knowledge, well let's just say they will be in for a rude awakening.

Thinking you know how to do everything from day one is a sure fire recipe for disaster and financial ruin. Knowledge has always been one of the absolute key ingredients for success in any field.

We will discuss more about the importance of knowledge and what is required to be successful in the real estate sales world in Secret #7.

The minute you think you know everything is the first minute of the end of your career. Some Realtors think that they are just too cool, or too smart, to attend training classes, seminars, conferences, read books, or even ask for advice. These Realtors better go find themselves a nice easy hourly job because there, someone will do the thinking for them!

There is a saying that it is the hunters that get paid because anyone can skin. In other words, having the ability to go out and get the business is where the money is made, not in the paperwork processing portion. The real estate sales business has many facets to it - all connected together like links in a chain. However there are two distinct sections to this chain. The first section of the chain contains the knowledge, activities and efforts needed to obtain leads (the hunter) and the second section of the chain focuses more on the knowledge of knowing how to process the leads (the skinner). As important as both of the sections are, I can guarantee you that the first portion is the hardest to achieve and build to a level that you will need to be successful in real estate sales.

The real estate sales business has always been a numbers game and always will be since it is virtually impossible to sell every house and every buyer that you generate.

The more transactions that you are involved in, and the more clients you work with throughout the year, the more experience and expertise you gain - which is beneficial for all concerned. You have to be in the game to be a valuable asset to yourself and your clients. Just like in sports, you cannot stand on the sidelines and expect to improve your game, generate sales, and grow your business. Become a hunter; get out there, generate the leads, and don't forget that when you do get a lead it is imperative that you do a great job from start to finish processing and working with that lead in order to obtain repeat and referral business. Don't wait until you think the time is perfect, until you are in a positive frame of mind, or when you feel the stars are aligned just right. Get into the game!

This reminds me of the story of two groups of people that were both asked to make the perfect clay pot.

Secrets of Success

The first group took on the challenge with the mindset that they were going to plan everything out first, start to finish, and be ultra-careful - working slowing and methodically.

This was to ensure that there were no mistakes on their way to producing the perfect clay pot. The second group just dove right in, working feverishly, with many a trial and error until they came up with the perfect clay pot.

In the end, the first group never really got off the drawing board. They were still in the planning stages, afraid to make a mistake, by the time the second group, who were not afraid to make a mistake, was now actively producing dozens of perfect clay pots daily.

The moral of the story is to get in the game and be involved. Go on open house tours, ask questions, learn and observe, network, and socialize with your fellow real estate agents. This can all be accomplished even if you don't happen to have any listings or buyers at the moment and it is all part and parcel of becoming successful in our industry. Even though a real estate sales career tends to attract the individualist, and the majority of Realtors do work on their own, real estate sales is actually a team sport, which we will discuss more at length in Secret #8.

I recommend that you read the book titled, *Ready, Fire, Aim* by Michael Masterson. This book talks about the idea that you can't wait until everything is perfect; you have to just take the plunge!

Every so often I will have a new or struggling Realtor approach me and start asking questions. But before I even begin to answer the first one, they launch into a long-winded tale of all the great things they have been doing and just how incredible they are as a Realtor.

Of course all those 'great things' have only produced 3 or 4 sales over the past 12 months. So it begs the question – "How is it working for ya?"

If you are a struggling Realtor, please just ask your question and then be quiet and listen to the answer!

Acting like you know everything is, well, just that - acting. Sooner or later (usually sooner than you think), the harsh reality hits home. With little or no sales, and lots of those pesky bills, you soon find yourself looking through the help wanted ads.

The best part about being in real estate sales is that you are your own boss. The worst part about being in real estate sales is also that you are your own boss! You have to shelve your ego and pride in order to find out what to do before you run out of money, because sooner or later the money will run out.

Top Realtors never stop learning and never stop asking questions. As a matter of fact, when you find yourself speaking to a top Realtor, you will realize that it will be them asking you questions - not the other way around. They know what they know and they are smart enough to find out what you know so they can add it to their portfolio. They do this all while keeping their ego and pride in check. Now don't get me wrong, ego and pride can be great motivators; but you have to learn how to control them, instead of letting them control you.

Last year, I had the opportunity to interview the top Realtor from my office, Donna Rooney. Donna and her team do an extraordinary amount of business, which earned her the number six spot in all of Canada for RE/MAX in 2011. Donna is dedicated to improving her knowledge and education every year. She achieves this by spending, not only thousands of dollars on coaching annually, but also by investing time and money in attending seminars and conferences, year after year. She does not do this because she has an endless amount of spare time; she does it because she knows that she has to in order to stay productive, effective, and at the top of her game.

Industry leaders believe in the obtaining of more knowledge to benefit themselves, their team members, and loved ones. In secret #7, we will discuss the key components of industry knowledge that, in turn, will assist you in the creation of your personalized business plan, Secret #9.

So the next time you are on a plane, say to yourself, "Gee, Ken was right. I don't know how to fly a plane. Good thing there is someone up front that does." Be glad that the pilot and co-pilot keep themselves up to-date and educated on their trade because all our lives depend on it.

The next time you find yourself at a house party and Sven is spouting off about re-arranging furniture and changing the wall coverings, followed by someone piping up and saying "Sven you should be a Realtor," try not to gag or strangle someone.

Secrets of Success

You have to accept the fact that the general public views our industry from the outside without understanding the complexity involved. Like all industries, it is always a whole lot different when you have to walk the talk.

When you are speaking to a struggling Realtor and they start out by asking you a question but, before you can answer, they launch into a 15-minute dissertation of all the wonderful things that they have been doing, ask them "How's it working for ya?"

Then, do your best to steer them in the right direction. Or, if you realize you are talking to a brick wall, you can just nod and smile! Now, if you find yourself speaking to a top Realtor, heed this same advice and listen to what they have to say. They clearly know something that allows them to enjoy the success they do!

Top Realtors know enough to know that they don't know! Do you?

Ken Eddy

Notes

_____

_____

_____

_____

_____

_____

_____

_____

_____

_____

_____

_____

_____

_____

_____

_____

_____

_____

_____

_____

_____

_____

_____

_____

_____

Notes

Secret #2

Ask the Right Question of the Right Person at the Right Time!

Now that you have realized how important knowledge is and you have accepted the fact that you need to "Know enough to know, that you don't know," it's time to move forward and track down answers. One way of doing this is to talk to the experts. This would include Realtors that have had tremendous success in one area or another because it just happens to be their forte. Nothing will advance your career and success faster than asking questions of these top Realtors because they can significantly shorten your learning curve.

In regard to being a successful Realtor, understand that the wheel has been invented along with practically every other tool, technique, system, and program that you will require to be successful. So there is no need for you to waste your time and money doing everything the hard way. This is not being lazy; it is working smart!

Step One

Write down the questions you want to ask. For example: What is your top source of business? (One of my personal favorites!) What should I pay my assistant? What kind of split do you have your buyer agent on? How do you stay in touch with your past clients? How do you handle a situation when someone wants to grind you down on your commissions? How do you get the listing at your price from day one?

As you can see, there can be a long list of questions in just about any category that you can think of in real estate sales. Get your list organized and prioritized so that when you are ready to ask your questions, you are logical, organized, and not bouncing all over the place.

Step Two

Locate the best person(s) to answer these questions for you. It could be someone in your office, a Realtor you meet at a convention or seminar, or even a speaker who has come to your office to present on various topics. You will find that it is good practice to ask two or three experts in each and every field that you are focusing on in order to get well rounded answers that take into consideration your budget, your experience, and your local market conditions.

For example, if you are trying to increase your social media-marketing program for your listings, there are individuals out there that have embraced social media and are utilizing it on a daily basis. You could speak to other Realtors in your office that have shown prowess at it and may be more tech savvy than you might be. This might mean picking the brain of someone half your age, but put that ego aside and be willing to learn! You can also attend seminars on the subject or even go online and search out advice from experts there.

As I write this, I am preparing to travel to San Francisco to host my annual Mastermind Retreat and I have a guest speaker who will be presenting on social media. I will be asking as many, if not more, questions than everyone else (and yes, I have written down my questions already).

Another good example involving a topic that we all have to become very good at in order to survive and thrive in our industry is past client retention. There is probably not one real estate office out there that does not have at least one past client retention expert. Virtually every speaker and trainer emphasizes the importance of staying in touch with your past clients. There is a wide variety of valuable sources for you to tap into via webinars, training sessions, books and, of course, asking questions in person of a top Realtor or speaker/trainer prior, during, or after a presentation. Having given many presentations over the years, I recommend that if you do not get the opportunity to ask your question during a presentation, email the questions in after the event. This way, the presenter can take their time to analyze your question, and maybe even do some research, to help formulate an answer that would be beneficial specifically to you.

Step Three

Make sure you ask the question at the right time. As you are trying to hunt down the answers, trying to build your personal real estate business, remember that everybody else is doing the same thing and they are focused on themselves. They do not sit around waiting for you to call them or walk into their office and ask your questions.

So, let's say that you have taken the time to write down a few key questions in regard to an area of real estate sales that you feel you need to improve on. Let's use the concept of Geographical Farming, which is marketing to specific areas/communities, as an example. Either in your real estate office, or another nearby one, you will find a Realtor who generates a lot of business from a specific geographical area. This could be a small sub-division of 500 homes to a large area of 10,000 homes; it can also be one particular condo project or even one main street.

Maybe you have spoken to this Geo Farming Guru before and they have mentioned to you how much business they generate from this particular source or perhaps you have noticed all their marketing and advertising material in a specific area for past few years.

These Realtors have become the neighbourhood experts and lots of sellers still prefer to use the local expert. I know this subject very well since I have been farming an area for over 24 years and am happy to say that I have generated hundreds of thousands of dollars from this source.

On this particular day, you find yourself walking through your office and there she is - the Geographical Farming queen. You say to yourself - "It's my lucky day! I have the right questions and here comes the right person." You ambush her in the hallway and then bury her with an avalanche of questions. Stunned, she will try to absorb what you have thrown at her and, in an effort to get away and get back to what she was focusing on before you interrupted her, she will likely just give you short quick answers to get rid of you - which may not help you much at all.

Now, you had the right questions and the right person, but you did not have the right time. They are all key points and each one as important as the other, but you have to combine them correctly.

Secrets of Success

If you truly want the expert to unveil to you their advice accurately and completely, be totally prepared – but don't pounce!

Attempting to corner someone at the office, or chat them up at a conference over a cocktail when there are several other people in attendance all vying for an audience with the guru, will be very ineffective. Now, I am not saying that you should not ask questions when you get a chance, but understand you will gain more insight by simply being prepared and timely.

Here is an example of a better approach:

Write down your questions, select the right person (in this case we will assume that the person is from your office), and then ask them if you could ask them a few questions on (state the topic) over coffee.

Now here is another hint for you: there are generally ten coffee breaks (Monday to Friday) and only five lunch breaks. Asking someone for coffee just about doubles your odds of getting him or her pinned down to a time. The problem with asking them to lunch is that they may already have a lunch routine. They may regularly eat at home (with their family), network with their own clients or spend the lunch hour at the gym.

You also have to be concerned what type of food they like, if they have food allergies, what is close by, and if you can you get a reservation. Not to mention the fact that you will probably have to be there at 11:45 to get a seat and tackle parking issues.

When you do arrive, there is too much wasted time between getting seated, ordering something to drink, chatting to the server, selecting a meal and eating it!

Pretty soon, your lunch is over and you have not even scratched the surface of your questions.

It makes more sense, and it is a more convenient, to take them for coffee, since these days there seems to be a Starbucks every 25 ft. You arrive, buy a coffee, sit down, and ask questions. You will easily have 30 minutes to 45 minutes of interruption free time to complete your Q and A, since nobody will walk up to you and ask you how the first few sips are tasting or interrupt you with other questions.

Throughout your real estate career, you should constantly ask questions. This is because, not only will you evolve and change, but so will the industry. Plus, as your business grows, new concerns and challenges will emerge. For example, when should you hire your first assistant? Which is the best past client retention system? Every step forward in your career will uncover new issues and concerns that you probably could have never imagined or considered before.

You need to seek clarity and direction, eliminate trial and error, and understand that the wheel has already been invented. So, why would you waste your time, money, and energy trying to build or invent a new system from scratch, when you could easily fast track it by asking the pros who have been where you currently are and are now where you want to be. These top Realtors can save you from making the same mistakes that perhaps they have made in their careers.

> **Smart people learn from their mistakes;**
> **a genius learns from somebody else's.**

I think back to when I first got into real estate sales - 25 years ago at the time of writing. Boy, if I could just step back in time and do one thing over (along with a few hundred other things!), I would have sought out more mentors and asked more questions on practically every topic in our industry, saving me an incalculable amount of time, energy, and money.

I would have spoken to more experts on geographical farming, open housing, past client retention, objection handlers, scripts, dialogues, and much more.

I have discovered in my career that top Realtors, the true professionals, have no problem in sharing their "Secrets of Success." You have to just get out there and ask in the right manner.

Be prepared with the right questions, select the right person, and be sure not to ambush them!

Top Realtors have learned to Ask the Right Question of the Right Person at the Right Time! Have you?

Notes

_____

_____

_____

_____

_____

_____

_____

_____

_____

_____

_____

_____

_____

_____

_____

_____

_____

_____

_____

_____

_____

_____

_____

_____

_____

Notes

Secret #3

Adapt and Change with the Times!

What worked yesterday does not necessarily work today! Now, the key word here is "necessarily". There are lots of things that worked yesterday that still work today, but there has been a tremendous amount of change over the past decade that truly has been unprecedented.

If you are newly licensed, you have the opportunity to start with a clean slate and, in some cases, even be ahead of the curve since you can jump right into what is working today not having to learn and then unlearn what worked before. You will also have the most current information instead of having to distinguish between old rules and new rules.

If you have just obtained your real estate license in the past year or so, this could quite possibly mean you have grown up with computers in the classroom and surfed the Internet since you were a kid and have no problem working the apps on your smart phone.

However, if you have been in the business for over 24 years, like I have, you have witnessed a long list of extraordinary changes that have taken place in our industry.

When I think back to the summer of 1988, when I launched into my real estate career, I am amazed and, in some cases, humoured by the changes. Here is a short list for your entertainment:

With the creation and adaption of the Internet, our ability to collect and share information quickly and easily has grown exponentially! How did we possibly survive without the web?

Let me tell you what you actually had to do to learn about a real estate sales career back in the dinosaur days.

Secrets of Success

You had to go to a library or a bookstore and hope to find some current real estate sales resources. If your real estate board was progressive, just maybe they might have a few books and tapes that you could sign out for a few days. That was it! If your local library did not happen to have a lot of relevant information, you were really out of luck.

Now, you can simply Google away to your heart's content and even download the books and resources that you require to use your Smart phone, iPad, Playbook, or Kindle (I am sure there will be ten more gadgets available by the time you read this) to work with at your leisure.

To conduct business with clients, we used to have to sit at a desk and use a desk phone (cord attached). This, of course, evolved to the fixed car phone (cord still attached) and then the big brick cell phone, then flip phones, and several other generations versus today's amazing smart phones. As I am proofreading and making some final adjustments, Apple just unveiled the new iPhone 5.

Our MLS system originally didn't allow for pictures- not even one! And when you glanced at the description, I can guarantee you that no one ever wrote a bad thing about their listing, so you had no choice but to drive out and personally view the listings.

This is whereas today, we have the option of adding a large album of pictures, virtual tours, digital postcards and electronic brochures.

Imagine you had to actually get in your car and drive out to the house just to see its exact location and surroundings (how prehistoric is that?) versus logging onto Google Earth via your smart phone without even leaving your desk, coffee shop, or any location. You can tour the sub-division with a bird's eye view, electronically walk up and down the street, and check-out the neighbour's homes, parks, and the rest of the community's facilities as you sip on your latte.

Advertising and marketing your listings generally consisted of placing ads in a newspaper, magazines, or your local real estate board rag (of course all of this was a colossal waste of money for the majority of Realtors) versus new low cost or free online and social media marketing - all helping to expose your listings instantly and literally around the world.

Personal brochures did your "hey have a look at me" promoting versus today's interactive websites and social media sites.

Back in the day, you actually had no choice but to call your clients or go to see them versus texting or emailing as we do today, if that is how they prefer to communicate with you.

Realtors' numbers were listed on the sign in the yard of each listing. This meant that people had to stop their car, write down your number and the address, then go home and call you from their land line versus your website address, text for info #s and QR codes.

There was one MLS system that was the keeper of all secrets, being the only access portal to the real estate world's listings versus a long list of websites (generally with information derived from the local MLS systems) available for everyone to surf any time they desire.

Organized real estate is at an interesting point in its long life, one of uncertainly and opportunity.

Today there are more discount brokerages out there then there has ever been in the history of organized real estate sales. The Internet has also given birth to a whole new generation of opportunists that see real estate as a quick and easy way to make some cash.

Sadly, we will have no choice but to bear this onslaught of discount brokerages as it cheapens the whole industry. Fortunately, their lack of professionalism and shortsightedness never last in our industry, just as get rich quick schemes never last in other industries.

This is true because if the client's concerns and needs are not the prime interest of the agent, the clients will soon realize this and eventually choose to hire true professionals to handle their real estate needs. A home is the biggest investment most people ever make and few would trust that process to a cheap, unprofessional agent.

Discount brokers are like the guy who shows up to a party with a bottle of cheap wine, then lurks around drinking everyone else's expensive wine and, at the same time, expecting everyone to drink his bottle of swill!

As an industry, we have to understand that our clients are more educated and have higher expectations than ever before. You have to ask yourself: are you running a business model based on a 20-year-old platform or are you running an up to-date model with all the new bells and whistles?

Get with the times or get left behind!

Top Realtors adapt and change with the times! Do you?

Ken Eddy

Notes

_____

_____

_____

_____

_____

_____

_____

_____

_____

_____

_____

_____

_____

_____

_____

_____

_____

_____

_____

_____

_____

_____

_____

_____

_____

_____

_____

_____

Notes

Secret #4

Take Care of Everything Inside your Four Walls!

In a nutshell, this Secret is about taking care of everything that is in your control. That means paying attention to everything in your business, not someone else's, and not wasting your time worrying about things that are out of your control.

I had a retail background prior to getting into real estate and I had worked my way up to be general manager of several large department stores across the country.

During this time, I certainly learned a lot in regard to the importance of organization, budgeting, time management, and the overall operation of a business.

My district manager would pop in every once in a while to review and evaluate both my performance and my store's performance. Now, I learned many a valuable lesson during these visits, but none more valuable than this: no matter how the local economy was performing, I was consistently reminded to "Take care of everything inside my four walls before I started worrying about things outside of my control like, most notably, the economy!"

There are things that are in your control and there are things that are not. The economy is definitely not! We are inundated daily with negative news about the economies of, not only our own country, but also of Europe, Japan, and dozens more. I can guarantee you, that no Realtor can control these economies, so quit worrying about them.

I have never forgotten the lesson, take care of everything inside your four walls, and I have done my best to implement it throughout my real estate career, taking care of the things that I can control and trying my best not to worry or let outside influences affect my decisions and actions.

This also applies to the status of other Realtors' businesses. If they are struggling and complaining, that's their problem - not yours.

Sure, you can give them some advice and direction but do not let them derail you. Don't let their struggles become your struggles; stay focused.

In my travels, I have encountered far too many people that have not learned this lesson. Imagine this: you arrive in a small, unknown town. Tired and hungry, you walk into the first restaurant that you spot. You seat yourself because no one is there to greet you and then you start to realize that the place is a bit of a dump; it is not as clean as you would hope, the food tastes rather bland, the service is painfully slow, and the prices are certainly not in line with the low level of everything else in the place.

On leaving the restaurant, you run into the owner and engage him in conversation. He gripes and moans about how the economy is killing his business! Now of course you are thinking, "How about cleaning up this pig pen, retrain the staff, improve the menu and then maybe your prices would be in line and business would not be so bad!"

I like using a restaurant as an example since I am sure that we have all had a similar experience.

It is crystal clear to all of us that, if the restaurant owner would take care of everything that is in his control ("everything inside of his four walls"), that his business would improve despite how the economy was performing.

If you cannot control it, don't worry about it! The restaurant owner cannot control the economy any more then we can. But, he has full control of everything else. His distraction with the things he can't control is inhibiting his ability to take care of his business and focus on growing it. If you can perform at a high level in a slow economy, think what you would do in a healthy economy!

This leads me to another story. It is called the Hot Dog Salesman. Now, I cannot remember when I first heard this story, but I know it was over 30 years ago and its lesson still rings true today.

An older gentleman had been selling hot dogs at his stand for years and doing very well.

He did so well, in fact, that he managed to make enough money to send his only son to college and, overall, to enjoy a pretty successful business. He had half a dozen choices of hotdogs and smokies and a wide assortment of condiments to choose from.

He had a sign above his hot dog stand and he also had signs at the end of the street, another one on the boulevard and yet another one on the nearby highway.

One day, his son returned home from college and was shocked to see that his dad had such a selection of products to sell as well as a wide-range of condiments plus expensive (albeit effective) signs all over the place. He immediately confronted his father and told him point blank, "Dad, do you not realize that there is a recession going on?! You cannot be spending all this money on signage and product! You will go bankrupt"!

Now, the Dad respected the fact that his son has a college education (after all he had paid for it). So he took down all the signs except the one above the stand, cut his selection down to a choice of just one hot dog, and kept only your basic ketchup, relish, and mustard condiments.

Within a few days people quit driving in from the highway and boulevard. Those that did were disappointed in the selection of product and toppings and ended up leaving dissatisfied.

Well wouldn't you know it, within weeks the old man's business dropped like a rock.

The father approached his son and said, "You know son, you are correct. There is a recession on." Now, the lesson to be learned here is pretty obvious. If you are going to rely on someone for advice, make sure they are qualified to give you that advice. Clearly, his son was not!

When you are in business, you have to recognize when and where to spend your money and when and where to cut back. You must know where to use your energy, your time, and your resources.

If you hit a bump in the road (and there will always be bumps - and sometimes craters), you have to be able to adapt, make adjustments, and control what is in your control.

Are you the restaurant owner who would rather bitch and whine about the economy instead of getting to work and doing what it takes to be successful? Or, perhaps, you are the hotdog salesman who listens to bad advice and stops doing what has been working for him so successfully over the years.

There will be times when you feel that the whole world is out to get you, nothing seems to be going your way, and you just can't catch a break. You find yourself longing for the good old days when things were easier and the economy was rocking. You think to yourself that if those good times would just come back, you could turn your business around. It is not only how you perform on the good days that count, it is also how you perform on the bad days that will make the difference between success and failure.

You cannot afford to just sit around and wait for the world to change, the stars to line-up, and all the ducks to be in a perfect row. Bad economy or not, these factors should never stop you from running your business properly.

Top Realtors take care of everything inside their four walls! What do you take care of?

Ken Eddy

Notes

_____

_____

_____

_____

_____

_____

_____

_____

_____

_____

_____

_____

_____

_____

_____

_____

_____

_____

_____

_____

_____

_____

_____

_____

_____

_____

_____

Notes

Secrets of Success

Secret #5

Use Your Strengths!

Your personal strengths will become key factors in your business success. Generally, if you are not very good at something, you tend to dislike it. Let's face it, if you hate doing something, do you really think that you will ever become good at it?

Become so good at your strengths that your weaknesses become insignificant!

I can hear a gigantic sigh of relief from you as you read this passage. You are saying to yourself, "Hallelujah! You mean I can quit beating myself up over not being good at something and focus on what I am good at?" Yes, that is 100% correct!

You first have to recognize your strengths and then incorporate them into your business.

I have broken the strengths down into three categories:

1. Core Strength- you are good at it and you should keep doing it.

2. Fixable- you are not bad at it, but it is important and so it demands your attention to fix and improve that skill.

3. Weakness- you are weak in that area, never have been good at it, and probably never will be. You are better to hire someone else to do it or just ignore it all together if you can.

Use your strengths and hire your weaknesses!

Go with your strengths!

This section is based on my research, using three books that are listed a few pages farther along as well as my own personal experiences and observations.

1. **Do you know your strengths?**

2. **Do you incorporate your strengths in your business on a daily basis?**

3. **Do you focus on your strengths?**

Or

1. **Do you focus on your weaknesses?**

2. **Are you constantly trying to fix your weaknesses?**

3. **Is the time you spend focusing on your weaknesses stopping you from devoting that precious time to work with your strengths?**

In school, what did you focus on? Was it your strengths or did you devote the majority of your time focusing on your weaknesses? Were you staying after school to focus on your strengths or was it to work on your weaknesses?

If you spend all your time focusing on your weaknesses, when do you think that you will you ever have the time to focus on and use your strengths?

A study completed with two groups of high school students had one group focus on a subject that they were weak in, let's give them 3 on a scale of 1 to 10 (10 being the best). Another group was asked to focus on a subject that they were relatively strong at, let's give them a 6 out of 10. Their teachers spent an extraordinary amount of time working with these two groups for the entire school year. At the end of the year, the group that was weak in the subject had managed to improve from a 3 to only a 4, whereas the group that started out stronger in the subject managed to improve the 6 to a 9! This proves that just because you devote a tremendous amount of time and energy focusing on one particular skill, it does not guarantee that you will be successful at it – especially if you dislike it in the first place.

But focusing on a subject that you like and have strength in, and are already doing a pretty good job at, means that you will improve even more.

Whatever you focus on becomes your reality! Many things in business demand and need your attention. In the end, it is up to you to decide what you should focus on and either thrive with it, fix, or improve that skill because it is an integral part of your business or choose to ignore/delegate it!

When you examine the rich and the famous, do you believe that they achieved that level of success and/or expertise by being pretty good at a lot of things or great at one thing?

I love this quote by the Jim Collins, author of the #1 International Bestseller *Good to Great*.

Good is the enemy of great.

Just being good at something, or a lot of things, will not get you to the top. It gets you to the middle or, maybe, if you are lucky, just a little above that. Here is an example of a couple of guys that achieved extraordinary success in their chosen fields:

Wayne Gretzky "The Great One"

In Wayne's long illustrious career playing professional hockey, he was awarded a basement full of trophies for his accomplishments. I won't list them all, but here are a couple of them:

- He won the Art Ross trophy, for winning the NHL's scoring championship, an astonishing 10 times!
- He won the Hart trophy, for being selected the NHL's Most Valuable Player, an amazing 9 times!

To say that Wayne was a pretty good offensive player would be one of the biggest understatements about professional sports. Wayne was not known and was never awarded trophies for being a defensive player (frankly nobody expected or cared if he did play defensively).

Secrets of Success

Wayne focused on his strengths and practiced his strengths from the first time he laced up a pair of skates in his backyard rink as a child in Brampton, Ontario. His strengths were scoring goals and setting up others to score; other players used their strengths to focus on the defensives needs of the team.

Another sports star that I am sure you are familiar with is Michael Jordan. He is one of the best, if not the best, basketball player to have ever walked onto a court. Michael led the Chicago Bulls to three straight NBA championships, which, needless to say, is a remarkable accomplishment. He then decided to apply his athletic ability to baseball. Now, Michael is a natural athlete to say the least, but baseball just wasn't his forte. He returned to the Bulls and led them to another three NBA championships in a row. Wow, now that is going with your strengths!

Wayne and Michael are world-class athletes. They recognized their strengths, they practiced those strengths and they exceled at them!

I like using sports personalities as examples. They are just like us Realtors. Everyone thinks they we are under worked and overpaid (until they try to do our jobs, of course).

What is strength?

When we think about ourselves, all of our characteristics, our personality traits, and our likes and dislikes how do we know what our strengths are? How can we recognize these strengths within ourselves?

With the help of the following books, and my own experiences, here is a method for understanding how you can have a serious look in the mirror to recognize your own strengths and weaknesses.

Strength Finder 2.0 by Tom Rath
Go Put Your Strengths to Work by Marcus Buckingham
Strengths Based Leadership by Tom Rath and Barrie Conchie

So, why is it that we become better and better at certain things? Why is it that you find yourself drawn in that direction? Maybe you think you are just following your nose, that it just comes natural to you.

The true reasons, like most things in life, are quite simple.

There are reasons, cause and effect, results, and patterns that follow us throughout our lives.

We gravitate toward some things and we pull away from others. We experience success and we suffer through failure. Nothing ever ends up affecting us the same as it does the next person. Do we inherit these so called strengths or do we learn them along the way? If your father was a great baseball player, does that mean that you also will become a great baseball player? You have his genes, you likely have grown taller and, perhaps, stronger than your father, but does that guarantee that you will excel in a particular area or have an interest in a subject because of your lineage?

Maybe he spent days coaching you along, year after year, practicing with you, showing you the ins and outs of the sport. Maybe he even sent you off to baseball camps and special clinics for you to hone your skills.

So which is it? Nature or nurture?

The truth of the matter is that it is approximately 50/50. Half of your God-given talents you inherited and the balance are due to nurture.

In other words, even though you have inherited a portion of your strength, the rest you learned, practiced, and improved upon throughout your life. When you think about your strengths, recognize and focus on those that can help you in your real estate career. The following are a few suggestions to get you started:

Organizer

Perhaps you have the ability to be a very organized person. Everything is in its place and planned out months in advance for you, if not years. You not only have a five-year plan, you have a ten-year plan! You make lists and stroke off each task as it is completed and sometimes you complete a task that was not even on the list, so you add it to the list just so you can stroke it off.

The opposite is the Tasmanian Devil type of personality that roars into the office, barking orders and throwing paper in every direction and then wonders why nothing gets done the way they thought they asked it to be. Plus they can never find what they are looking for or remember where they might have left it.

They are constantly late (personally, this drives me nuts) and are perplexed why they never seem to get anything completed on time. Does this remind you of anyone? Perhaps the person in the mirror?

Detail Person

Nothing gets by you. Your mind is like a steel trap. Your planning skills are second to none. Had you worked at NASA, they would never have had to stop a countdown. As a Realtor you have every detail of every listing that you are marketing from who built it, when it was built, type of windows, thickness of carpet, and even right down to the last time the furnace was cleaned. You never have to get back to people since you know all there is to know about that listing when they first ask you.

No one questions your mathematical skills; they accept that your calculations on price, mortgage, and closing costs are bang on (just for the record, if you possess this unique strength, you are a rare breed for a Realtor and good on you - I wish I was better at the details) and why would they not be correct? Anything else would be inexcusable as far as you are concerned.

Big-Picture Person

You're not just going to sell one condo; you are going to sell the whole building. As a matter of fact, the company that owns the building will be using you to liquidate all of their holdings. While some Realtors struggle from one sale to another with the details seemingly consuming all their time and energy, the big-picture Realtor is busy working on next month's marketing program and calculating how they can increase their sales and profit over the next few years. Perhaps they will buy the office or maybe even the region. Nothing is too big for them to contemplate!

People Person

Your spouse, girlfriend, or boyfriend, loves having you along at company parties and gatherings. You don't go hide in the corner and stare at your watch. You have that unique ability to bring down someone's defensive walls and you can chat with them on a personal level, creating mutual trust. In the sales world, when everything else is equal, consumers will gravitate toward, and do business with, people they like and feel confident referring business to that person as well.

Being a People Person is a handy trait to have in our industry. Two good friends of mine in the industry can certainly be described as People Persons; they are John Humphreys and Leo Bruneau. Both of these gentlemen can hold conversations and put people at ease in a manner of minutes.

The have recognized that being a People Person is a strength they have and they utilize that strength on a daily basis.

Leader

Perhaps you do not think of yourself as a leader, as a person that other people look up to and respect. This is a trait that only a few have and, surprisingly, most do not realize that they are leaders, albeit in some cases, reluctant ones. In this situation, it is as important to know what others think of you, just as it is important to understand what you think of yourself. As humans, we all need some form of leadership and if you possess that strength, don't be shy about using it. Good leaders have the ability to take into consideration everyone's wants, needs, and desires. They adapt and adjust, making sure that they lead everyone, not just the disciples. This differs from the "my way or the highway" type of leader because, again, real estate sales takes a team effort and someone who is unyielding or unwilling to work with others will not last.

The Eternal Optimist

Being the glass half full type of person is a true strength. It can be the tipping point in so many situations. You could sway decisions one way or the other with your positive attitude, making or breaking deals, or even effecting larger events in your life and the lives of others. A pessimistic Realtor may confuse their clients with their negative attitude and even affect fellow Realtors, perhaps swaying them away from a new marketing strategy or attending a training event or conference, claiming that it would be a waste of time and money. A positive Realtor, on the other hand, will show support and offer advice to help enhance the new marketing strategy and agree that attending the conference would be very beneficial. When you lose a listing to someone else, the pessimist Realtor falls into a funk for weeks. They cannot comprehend how that seller could have possibly hired another Realtor. They continue to waste their time and energy fretting and complaining.

An optimistic Realtor, however, looks at it with a different perspective. For example, they may say to themselves, "What can I learn from that situation" or they may say, "Well at least I will have more time to spend with my other clients and focus on getting more clients. Besides, when the listing expires I will be the first one they call back to get it sold"!

Bridge Builder or Mediator

Are you the person called upon to break up office arguments? Do you have that uncanny ability to see both sides of the story and eventually calm the waters? We need these people, not only in our offices, but also sometimes in our own family. (Hmm, that may have been the reason my parents always sat me between my brother and sister on long road trips).

I have always said that a Realtor is the glue that is needed to bring two warring parties together. Buyers and sellers are vying for the polar opposite outcome during each and every transaction. Your job as a Realtor is to bridge this gap and help create a win/win situation. This strength really comes in handy when working with a married couple that have a difference of opinion when it comes to the perfect house. You would be amazed at the fights I've witnessed between couples. So, the ability to bring together two individuals whose ideas are very different is indeed an asset in any industry.

Researcher

Some people have the natural ability to concentrate, dig into, and devote the necessary time in order to uncover the material they require. So for all you ADD people out there, you can breathe a big sigh of relief, for you can hire someone who has the patience of Job to do all of your meticulous time consuming research. Yes, there are people out there for whom research is right up their alley. Thank goodness, for many of us find it quite tedious! And a note of caution for all you researchers: don't get too caught up in digging for details if you should be dedicating more time to networking and other aspects of the industry. You can't grow your business by staying in your office and researching everything to death 24/7.

In order to ascertain your specific personal strengths, complete this simple exercise:

Write down a few strengths that you believe you possess. This may take you a bit of time, so reflect back on the list above and think about yourself. Which of those traits do you have? Generally, this type of introspection is an activity that we as humans rarely do. But you will discover that knowing your personal strengths will help you shape your future.

Your strengths:

- _____

- _____

- _____

- _____

- _____

How did you make out? Did you manage to recognize and write down a few of your strengths or did you find it tough? Don't be surprised if it was a little harder than you thought it would be, since most people do not know their own strengths.

Now who do you think knows you best? Your family, your peers, or the kids you grew up with? Surprisingly, it is often your peers that tend to know you best.

Asking your peers to name your strengths may reveal them, or at least bring them to the forefront of your thoughts, because you simply may not have been paying attention to them or never took the time to really think about what they might be. A peer may say to you that they believe one of your strengths is that you are a natural leader. Maybe you never thought of yourself as a leader, but by someone mentioning it, you start to use this newly discovered strength.

Secrets of Success

Once you have recognized your strengths, you can focus on them, improve them, and incorporate them into your business. You will find this much more enjoyable and productive than spending all your valuable time slugging it out with your weaknesses!

Remember: Become so good at your strengths that your weaknesses become insignificant!

Top Realtors use their strengths and hire their weaknesses! What do you use?

Ken Eddy

Notes

_____

_____

_____

_____

_____

_____

_____

_____

_____

_____

_____

_____

_____

_____

_____

_____

_____

_____

_____

_____

_____

_____

_____

_____

_____

_____

_____

_____

Notes

Secrets of Success

Secret #6

Personal and Professional Development!

Top Realtors believe in and embrace personal and professional development. They are constantly educating themselves, improving upon skills, and sometimes replacing the core fundamentals by working on the basics to make themselves even more successful.

Oh, I can hear your thoughts right now, "Boy this is this going to be a bunch of boring talk about taking care of the basics and the basics will take care of you. Count your pennies and the dollars take care of themselves. Slow and steady wins the race". That's the type of crap that I am sure that you have heard a thousand times over, right?

If you close down your ears (or in this case, don't read this section) your entire business is going to collapse no matter what else you do. This is where most Realtors fail; they try to jump 10 spaces down the board and then are surprised when they lose the game.

Recently, I was reminded by a Realtor in my office, of the first speaker I went to listen to 20 years ago. Oddly enough, that very same speaker is back here in Calgary giving a presentation while I was writing this book. The young Realtor asked me if it would be worth his time to attend the presentation. I hardly knew where to start, but of course, I advised him to attend.

When I had first heard this same speaker years ago, one of his very first comments was, "I bet you that there are people at your office that told you not to come today. That all you were going to accomplish was that you would just return to the office with this happy glow on, be all pumped-up, but you really did not learn anything and in a day or so, you would be right back to where you started so why waste your time going?"

When I did return to my office, that is exactly what one of my fellow Realtors said to me.

He is no longer in the business and it is not because he had enough money to retire, if you get my drift!

Do not listen to these negative people just because they think that they are so smart or perhaps have grown lazy and think that they do not need to attend training presentations to improve their skills. Do what is best for you, not them.

Yes, I know some Realtors think that they are the best thing that has happened to real estate sales since the invention of the MLS system. But if your plan is to build a solid, profitable, long-term business, then completing and maintaining a solid foundation, ensuring that the basics are covered is what everything else is built on.

Obviously you have continued to read, so here is the plan:

By now, I am sure you agree that every business is built from the ground up - on solid foundational blocks.

These foundational blocks are universal and can be found supporting almost every successful business out there.

We all want to make money. We all want to be out there selling the million-dollar plus homes and hauling in the big bucks. But, that is the end of a long process and for every end there is a beginning. As we complete the construction of your foundation level of your business, we are actually completing the beginning. As much as you want to gallop ahead, you have to pull in the reins and take care of the fundamentals or your career will be short lived.

The following are a list of building blocks for the foundation that you will need to address, add, repair, or replace.

Positive Attitude

Greet each day, each event, and each obstacle with a positive attitude, as it is your very first step to success! Looking at the world with a glass half full approach will fill your life with choices, but viewing the world with a glass half empty will do nothing but limit your opportunities.

Having a positive attitude is a choice, because I can tell you for certain that you do not wake up in the morning automatically having a negative attitude. I like to think you wake up in neutral and from there you make your choice. Adopting and maintaining a positive attitude will help you look at the day seeing a whole world of possibilities.

If you think you can do a thing or think you cannot do a thing, either way you are right.
-Henry Ford

Doors will open for you, opportunities will arise out of nowhere, people will want to associate with you, and solutions to problems will appear.

Of course, we all know the "Yeah, but" people. These are the people that no matter how positive a situation you outline to them, they will tend to agree and disagree with you in the same short sentence…

"Yeah…but…what about this or that, maybe we should not even try it, what if they won't give it to us, if we fail then we would have to start all over, I'm going to have to think about it".

The world is full of these people and I feel sorry for them. They can see the light at the end of the tunnel, but they do not have the gumption to walk toward it. Sadly, they find it easier just to stick with the status quo and continue on with the same old, same old. Make a choice to be positive every day. It is always better than the alternative!

Support from Family and Friends

Wow! If there is a keystone in your foundation, here it is. Having support from your loved ones is very important to your success, but unfortunately sometimes it takes a while to win them over, to get them to see your vision, and to understand that the sacrifices of today equal the rewards of tomorrow.

As much as having everyone in your corner from day one would be extremely beneficial, understand that it may take some time. Eventually, though, when you do win them over, your career will soar to heights that it just could not have reached without their support and backing. Be patient with them, as it will pay off for everyone.

Secrets of Success

Assertiveness

We have all heard the Nike slogan… "Just do it!"

Being "assertive" is a human characteristic that can separate you from the pack. The moment they run into a slight speed bump, the majority of people will throw in the towel, stating "it is just too hard to continue because if there is one speed bump, well there sure as heck will be another so why even try"!

One thing that I have realized over the years is that the harder something is to do, the less competition you will have. When you find yourself running into a roadblock, it is best to adopt the attitude of "this is great because I know that half my competition will quit now because this will be too hard for them to over-come".

Assertiveness is a particular mode of communication. Dorland's Medical Dictionary defines assertiveness as: a form of behavior characterized by a confident declaration or affirmation of a statement without need of proof; this affirms the person's rights or point of view without either aggressively threatening the rights of another (assuming a position of dominance) or submissively permitting another to ignore or deny one's rights or point of view.

During the second half of the 20th century, assertiveness was increasingly singled out as a behavioral skill taught by many personal development experts, behavior therapists, and cognitive behavioral therapists. They knew that assertiveness is often linked to self-esteem and is a key component of success.

Note: I am not talking about being aggressive; as a matter of fact, being aggressive can do you more harm than good. It cannot only destroy the relationship with your client but also with your fellow Realtors.

To be aggressive is to exhibit behaviors intended to cause pain or harm against members of one's own species, or towards another species. Predatory behavior of members of one species towards another species is also described as "aggressive."

To exhibit aggressive behavior towards members of another species is common, such as in these examples: "Lions are aggressive hunters of antelopes," and "Eagles are aggressive hunters of small mammals."

See, you don't really want to be labeled as an aggressive person, do you?

Also I would like to point out that you should always remember to protect your reputation and your professional image when dealing with other Realtors. Not only is it the nice thing to do, but it is also the smart thing to do. You will likely be doing several transactions with that particular Realtor throughout your career. Wouldn't it be wise to have a respectful non-confrontational relationship when dealing with that Realtor and others?

Organizational Skills

Organization is a skill that many Realtors simply do not have. It tends to run against the grain of human traits that most Realtors actually do have.

Utilizing organizational skills that will help you map out your career, structure your schedules, assist in the design of a marketing plan, and select the path for your own education and the training of your staff. Plus, practically every other aspect of our industry is so important that if you cannot do it, hire someone to do it for you.

A good friend of mine, Les Benczik, from Toronto, Ontario exemplifies organization. Throughout his career, Les has taken charge of his education; he has planned out which courses to take, which trainers to hire, and when to move on to the next level. Les is a master of time management and delegation. He has built a world class team of professionals and as much as Les would give them all the credit for how smooth the team runs, I know it takes a true leader to pull it all together.

Of course, due to the nature of real estate sales, it generally does not attract the organized type of individual; it tends to attract more of the Tasmanian Devil personalities that I referred to earlier. If you feel that perhaps you have an unorganized little devil inside of you, don't despair; help is just a phone call away.

You can hire someone in the form of an assistant or coach that can help you get and stay organized, on track, and on time. They can assist in the organization of your team as well and guide you to the right training programs and seminars that are focused on what you need to learn or that you may have to adapt and work on at that present time in your career.

In some cases, even a business partner or office manager that has organizational skills in aces may be a necessary addition to your team.

Communication Skills

Communication skills are critical to a person's success, no matter which industry they happen to find themselves employed in. There are over a 171,000 words in the English language, so understanding and practicing the use of even a small portion of them is very helpful during your day-to-day communication with others. Being a good communicator will do nothing but enhance your other skills.

Again, as mentioned earlier, being a good communicator is a strength that some people have and others struggle with, but we all have to focus on it and improve because we all have no choice but to use our communication skills on a daily basis.

The fact that communication is 8% verbal, 37% vocal, and 55% visual does not leave a lot of leeway to work with if your communication plan calls for just texting and emailing everyone that you deal with on a day-to-day basis.

It imperative that you discover which method of communication your clients prefer and make the necessary adjustments. If you expect everyone to adhere to "your" system of just texting or emailing, when "you" feel it is important, think again! Be smart; be flexible!

Perhaps this is your forte. You pick up languages like nobody else, you understand how to engage others to make them feel comfortable, and you have no problem getting your message conveyed.

If you have the command of several different languages, this could open your business up to work with new immigrants that feel more comfortable when dealing with someone with whom they can communicate easily.

Take note of this previous passage because if you have moved to your city/country from a foreign land and have the ability to speak two or three different languages, I highly recommend that you take advantage of this ability.

For example: If you are fluent in Hungarian, Polish, Mandarin, or any other language make sure you have this noted on your profile on your company's website, your website, your promotional material, and on your business cards.

Just this week, I received an email through a social media site that a lot of my fellow Realtors at my office are part of, asking if anyone knew of a Realtor that could speak Iranian. Unfortunately, I did not know anyone that does speak Iranian but I am sure that there are Realtors in my office that do and because they don't let others know about it, they miss these types of opportunities.

Reading, writing, listening, or simply just holding a two-way conversation, are skills that seem to be waning and even on the edge of extinction. With permission, I have re-published an article composed by John Cadley, a copywriter from Syracuse, New York. John writes a rather humorous, but very true article on the lack of communication skills of the younger generation. His comments and views on today's young communicators are priceless and, sadly, accurate.

Imagine a tech savvy person who is proficient in gaming, texting, and emailing - who has no problem whatsoever communicating with their friend's day or night - heading off for their first interview.

Below is an excerpt from the June 2011 Toastmaster magazine:

So, Um, You Know, Here's, Like My Column, Ya Know?

We have a generation of college graduates who treat the English language like a rented mule. They push, prod and poke it into submission for the lowly purposes of texting, emailing and tweeting. Never mind the millions of years it's taken for human speech to evolve into a wondrous system of nuance and complexity. We now have an entire generation that would rather communicate like birds on a telephone wire.

The rules of spelling, grammar and punctuation are not simply ignored; they're beaten with a stick. Language has no intrinsic beauty. On the rare occasions when technology fails and these bright young minds must use the spoken word, they use a vocabulary so flea-bitten with "um," "uh," "like," you know" and "sorta" that it does, in fact, resemble the muted braying of a barnyard animal.

Secrets of Success

This is the future, ladies and gentlemen: intelligent young men and women who can master complex video games, program TiVo from their cell phones, control home appliances from their laptops, write computer code in their sleep, even graduate with honours - but who can't spell "restaurant."

As a lover of language, I am deeply saddened. As an employer seeking to hire individuals who can express themselves clearly, I am scared out of my wits. I have nightmares of hiring a recently minted graduate and sending her out on a client presentation. The room is filled with people who could well determine the fate of my business, and standing there before them is…Snooki from the U.S. reality TV show Jersey Shore:

"So, like, yeah-it's, like, way cool that you're all here and I'm, you know, like, just sayin'- this is cool."
You're here to present the marketing plan for 2011, is that correct?"
"Yeah"
"What is it?"
"We gotta sell more stuff."
"What's your strategy for doing that?"
"You know, just, like, do stuff that makes people want to buy it, you know? Like, commercials and stuff."
"What kind of commercials?"
"With stuff in it."
"What else?"
"You know, like, ads and stuff in really serious, important magazines like, you know, Vogue and Glamour. And then, you know, like Facebook and Twitter with lots of bling bling about how this stuff is great and how you buy it and tell all your friends' cause they're gonna freak that they don't have it so they'll run out and get it and text everybody with pictures and stuff and then everybody'll be flippin' to buy it and you'll sell more stuff.
You know, like that, Just sayin'."

It's at this point that I wake up in a cold sweat and read a few pages of Shakespeare to reassure myself that real language has, in fact, not been annihilated during the night by an ICBM missile from New Jersey armed with monosyllables.

It's unfortunate that these young turks have to write a resume, try as they might to appear witty and articulate, what should be a list of qualifications often turns into a litany of disqualifications.

Let's start with applying for a job as a proofreader and actually misspelling the word. Really? Then let's make sure we actually do proofread that resume to avoid saying that previous work experience includes "stalking, shipping and receiving," or that we were "instrumental in ruining the entire Midwest operation of a major chain store," or that we spent a summer in a call centre "taking odors."

We might also want to run the spelling and grammar functions on our computer – heaven forbid we could actually refer to a dictionary – to make sure we don't request a salary "commiserate with our experience," or that we don't opine on how we feel our substantial qualifications will prove "detrimental to our future success."

Logic and specificity help, too.

Saying you're a 'hard worker, etc." isn't really a list of qualifications. And it's nice that your twin sister has a degree in accounting, but that doesn't tell us much about you, does it?

Also, just for the record, being bi-lingual in three languages may be impressive, but it doesn't say much for you math skills. And finally, when I ask how large the department was that you worked in as a summer intern, "three storeys" isn't the answer I'm seeking.

I know you're smart and capable. I know you'll perform well and do your parents and your employers proud. But come on, kids – would it kill you to learn how to spell restaurant?

Have I made you think about your last few conversations, perhaps some flashbacks to an interview from your past, or how about that last home evaluation that you recently completed? As much as we all believe that we have an excellent command of the English language and feel that we do a flawless presentation each and every time, maybe it is time to re-evaluate your communication and presentations skills.

If you feel this way, I highly recommend Toastmasters to each and every one of you. A great Toastmaster club will help you build confidence and help you think on your feet, allowing you to make your presentation to clients smoother and more precise. It will help you to improve your body language, tonality, and assist in expanding your vocabulary.

To find more information about Toastmasters and Toastmaster clubs in your area, log onto www.toastmasters.org.

How about answering the phone? What is with so many people thinking that they are too busy to answer the phone when it rings? I have heard many speakers exclaim on stage, "Busy people don't answer calls; they return calls".

Now that is all fine and good - if you want to live with the consequences. What happens when two, so-called "busy" people actually want to get hold of one another? They never will because each of them feels that they are too busy to answer the phone!

A long time friend of mine, and one of the top Realtors from my office, John Linster, has said for years, "The phone is a cash register; when it rings, answer it". You spend a lot of time and money trying to attract business, so don't make it hard for your potential clients to get a hold of you!

Resilience

Definition: *The ability to recover quickly from illness, change or misfortune; buoyancy.*

We all know the hard luck cases in your office that always seem to have a black cloud hovering over their heads. All too often, they will corner you in the office and force you to listen to the long version of a short story of how they lost a listing to another Realtor or some other traumatic event that has absolutely ruined their day. In fact, forget the day. They will claim that the whole month has just become the worst month of their life and it will probably screw up the entire year!

Unfortunately, it is not going to be the last time that you have to hear this same story because every time you run into them, either in the office or out in the parking lot, you are subjected to the same story and the same non-stop whining over and over.

Of course, you just politely stand there nodding and pretend you are listening. But secretly, you are praying that your cell phone rings with a call that you absolutely have to take just as an excuse to get the heck out of there.

The whiny Realtor has to learn to get over it, take in on the chin, and move on. You are not going to win every battle, get every listing, or sell a home to every client. There is a hockey analogy that states, "If you score every time you shoot the puck at the net, you are not shooting enough".

The same can be said for real estate sales; if you list every house that you do a market evaluation on, you are not going on enough market evaluations. If you sell every house that you list, you are not listing enough houses. If you sell a home to every buyer you work with, you are not working with enough buyers!

Be resilient, bounce back quickly, learn from your mistakes and misfortunes, and move on. In other words…Get over it and get over it quickly!

Professionalism

Ok, you are presenting an offer to a couple of your best friends and you are acting (appropriately) very professional. What are the consequences?

A. They appreciate your professionalism and the fact that you are treating them with such respect, even though you are great friends.

B. They laugh and joke about how professional you are acting and then tell you that you don't have to be so uptight and careful around them and they insist that you loosen up.

Now, let's say that you adopt the attitude of, "heck, these are some of my best friends, and they really don't care if I show up in shorts, act like we are all going to a BBQ together and then casually outline the offer or other details." What could be the consequences?

A. That is cool with them and everything proceeds along nicely.

B. They are extremely offended that you are treating them with such a casual attitude, the transaction collapses, and not only do you lose the deal, but you also lose a pair of longtime friends.

I would encourage you to walk on the professional side of the line, just to be safe - take the jokes if you have to! They will continue doing business with you and recommend you to others because you treated them with respect. However, if their boss or someone they respect asked for a recommendation and they picture you in your shorts and sandals and acting unprofessional and careless the last time they dealt with you, do you really think they will offer your name up as a good Realtor? Probably not - even if they are your best friends.

A person's opinion of you is formed in the first 3 seconds of your meeting them. Since there cannot be a do-over, you want to ensure that you make a good first impression because it could be a long up-hill battle to change a bad first impression.

This brings us to "dressing for success." It is a saying that we have all heard time and time again. Why? Because it is true. Why handicap yourself right out of the gate by dressing like a slob?

It is like being late for an appointment. Oh, you probably are thinking, "heck I was only a few minutes late…" No you weren't; you were late, period. Now you have to dig yourself out of that hole just to get back to ground level.

I have never liked the saying "Fake it until you make it". It sounds underhanded, like you are trying to put one over on someone else. But I do like this saying from fellow Canadian and Olympian Cary Mullen:

Act like a champion, until you are a champion.

I believe this quote is a much better reflection of the attitude it takes to succeed. Champions tend to always act with style, grace, and professionalism. Why not do that from the start and then, when you feel that you have made it, all you have to do is continue acting the same way?

It is true that you sometimes have to "put the cart in front of the horse," meaning that there are times in your life when you have to spend a few dollars on dressing a little better, driving a little nicer car, and acting like you are enjoying slightly more sales success then you currently are. People will sympathize and console someone that is struggling, but they would rather do business with someone who is doing well and whom they deem to be successful. Everyone wants to work with a winner and associate with professionals.

My friend, Greg Hamre from Ottawa, has always been an impeccable dresser. Even when Greg is taking his son to a hockey practice in the early evening, he is dressed for success. Everyone that runs into Greg, whether he is at the rink or in the office, has the immediate impression that he is a professional and, as I said previously, people want to do business with professionals. Now, I am not advocating that you always have to be dressed impeccably, with pen in hand ready to write a contract.

Just remember, however, that in our industry you are almost always on stage; your clients, possible clients, and the public's opinion of you can translate into a deal or into no deal. This is true no matter if you are shopping for groceries, going to a child's event, or attending a party.

You don't have be in a three-piece suit at every function, but you want to be aware that how you act and how you look for it will always be evaluated. Dress appropriately; dress for success!

Self-Esteem and Self-Confidence

Generally, self-esteem and self-confidence are two things that you want to acquire early on life - but not everyone does. The good news is that this is a part of your own personal growth that you can focus on and improve.

Self-esteem is defined as: having a stable sense of personal worth or worthiness.

Self-confidence, on the other hand, is defined as: having a belief in yourself, the belief that you have the ability to do things well or deal with situations successfully.

We all know people, or even ourselves, that have struggled with self-esteem. You may have had to start when you were young and build it step-by-step though-out your life.

Self-confidence is also something that can be built one success at a time. I like to say, "Celebrate small victories for they are the stepping-stones to big ones." These small victories can help us to build confidence and the more confidence you have, the easier and more frequent your victories will be.

Getting that first listing, successfully negotiating your first transaction, and the smooth handling of an objection are all stepping-stones to even larger successes. Each and every time you win a battle, no matter how small it is, will help build self-esteem and self-confidence.

Secrets of Success

All of us as Realtors have to be on guard and recognize people that can undermine our self-esteem and self-confidence - and then do our best to stay clear of them. There are a lot of people that you may know that would like to see you successful, just not too successful, because they assume that your success might make them look bad.

I'll warn you now that some of these people might be your co-workers, close friends, or even some family members. This is especially true if they have always done better than you financially. When your business really takes off, there could be some tension; but again, if you act with the style and grace of a champion, eventually they could be your biggest supporters.

Enthusiasm

Enthusiasm is contagious. Be a carrier.

-Susan Rabin

During my many talks with top Realtors from around North America, they have admitted to me that keeping their enthusiasm can be a pretty tough after years and years of having to perform at the top of their game. However, in the same breath, they confirm that being enthusiastic about your career is crucial to one's success.

I have struggled with keeping my enthusiasm more often than I care to remember and one of the ways that I combat it is to attend conferences.

I have found, and many of my colleagues feel the same way, that by attending a conference or seminar, the positive atmosphere can re-ignite the fire and passion that we all desperately need to perform at the top of our game.

Enthusiasm has turned the tide in many a championship game; it creates more victories with heart than with talent and when applied to an uncertain occupation like real estate sales, it can be the difference between success and failure.

This means not focusing on the negative events and people around you. I've talked about this before, but sometimes when there are others spouting off negative complaints, its human nature to want to join in. Believe me, I know how easy it is, especially if you've had a rough week or rough month.

But you have to recognize it for what it is because awareness is the first step to getting out from under the dark cloud. Go back and read that book that set you on fire or listen to something inspirational if there isn't a conference to attend and force yourself to be around positive, successful people - even if you find it slightly intimidating!

When things were not going all that well for me in those early years, one of the hardest things to do was listen to the successful Realtors talk about their many sales, listings, and buyers that they were working with. But, enthusiasm absolutely is contagious and the only way to catch it is be around those that have things going on.

Force yourself to bask in their positivity and try your best to soak it in instead of being irritated. Soon, you will find that positive attitude seeping into your day and reflecting nicely in your business.

Accept Criticism

With seven billion people in the world, you have to accept that not everyone is going to have the same opinion or look at things the same way as you do - so get used to it.

When you ask for advice and feedback, absorb it, digest it, and act on it. Remember, there are at least two types of criticism: solicited and unsolicited; both have their merits and value.

Solicited Advice: You have asked a person for advice that has in-depth knowledge and experience on the subject or has an abundance of common sense that you can rely on. In addition, they are the type of person that will give you direct, well-structured, and unbiased opinions. Now you may have selected the person you wish to give you advice or the right person just happens along at the perfect time.

Unsolicited Advice: "Oh...I was just trying to be helpful." How many times have we heard that? Generally, unsolicited advice is just one thing: criticism and criticism only.

Fortunately there is something to be learned from these blunt and direct comments such as the advantage of having an uncensored opinion of you and/or what you are doing or who is jealous of your success. Possibly it brings a viewpoint that you never would have considered, even if the person is uneducated on the subject. In fact, it just might be the sobering comment that you needed to hear. Do not let this type of advice derail you or erode your confidence; perhaps you could take the unsolicited advice to a mentor and ask their opinion to get a balanced perspective.

As humans, we are constantly downloading information, filtering it, and trying to discern which pieces of advice we will take or not take. At the end of the day, it is up to you to take it or leave it.

You may either absorb it or let it bounce off of you. It's your choice as to how you will let it affect you, good or bad.

Discipline

In real estate sales, nobody is going to kick you out of bed in the morning and herd you off to work, so you better have the self-discipline to do it yourself. Discipline for a Realtor is like oxygen to an athlete; you can perform with a little bit of it, but you can thrive on a lot of it! Here again this is about being as effective as possible with the time that you dedicate to work, so you can have more time off to enjoy with family and friends. This is not about packing the maximum of work into every single second of the day. Discipline is consistency and commitment – not hundreds of push-ups per day!

When the alarm clock goes off, it's easy to think, "Oh crap, it is just too darn early to get up," and hit the snooze button, repeatedly, until, eventually, you just give up and turn it off. After all, you are your own boss; you set your own hours and you congratulate yourself for showing a house late in the evening last week so you deserve to sleep in – right? When you finally struggle out of bed at 10am, your phone rings with an offer of golf in mid-afternoon. You say to yourself, "Why not? The day's half over anyways and, heck, I can make a fresh start in the morning".

Is this you or perhaps someone you know? You need to have discipline in your life, not only to get out of bed in the morning, but even the discipline to follow-up on a lead, call a past client, attend a meeting, show up to appointments on time - the list goes on.

Paul Mair was the founder and co-owner of RE/MAX Real Estate Central, the #1 RE/MAX office worldwide. This office has completed more transactions annually than any other office world-wide for RE/MAX for the past 13 years straight.

Paul has recently sold his half of the company to his business partner, but during his ownership days, and even today, Paul will tell you that two of the key characteristics that a Realtor must possess if he or she wants to be successful in this industry are Discipline and Respect.

Respect

R.E.S.P.E.C.T. Just like the song by Aretha Franklin. Respect for your client, your fellow Realtors and for yourself makes my list of foundation building blocks that are necessary to succeed in any industry.

The minute we start treating anyone with a lack of respect is the moment we stop respecting ourselves. There is an old saying, "You sleep in the bed you make" and showing limited or no respect to practically everyone, sooner or later, comes back to haunt you.

This goes for your fellow real estate agents as well. Far too often, we run into another Realtor that firmly believes that they are the best thing since sliced bread and everyone has to kowtow to their schedule. They feel that they do not need to call you to cancel a showing, or that our clients should just be happy that their clients have even written an offer. You get the picture. So, don't be like that; be respectful because we are all in this together and you know another old saying, "What goes around, comes around".

Be respectful to yourself and others. Show up when you say you are going to. When someone is waiting for you and you consistently show up late (how many acquaintances do you have that act like that) it shows the other person that you have no respect for their time.

That person that you continue to disrespect may be polite and say, "no problem" and continue on as if everything is fine, but trust me, it is not, and your tardiness will come back to bite you in the butt when others start to treat you the same way as you have been treating them (sounds like the golden rule to me).

Here is a saying I made up years ago, "Don't mistake politeness for naiveté." In other words, they may be nice, but they are keeping score and if you don't honour your word the points are not going in your favour.

Self-Starter

Without repeating half of the Discipline trait, I will only add this: being a self-starter is a trait that you better have if you truly want to excel in the real estate sales world. You cannot wait for someone to tell you what to do, how to do it, or when to start doing it. It has to be the person in the mirror that is doing the starting - not someone else. Don't spend all day procrastinating; take the first step, then the next, and so on and so on. Remember, ready, fire, aim!

Multi-Tasking

If we all had an endless amount of time to devote to each and every task that we had to tackle day after day, boy would we do a great job. Unfortunately, that is not how business works. Situations can pop-up out of nowhere with little or no notice, priorities can shift like the wind, schedules don't coincide perfectly with yours, computers will lock-up, deadlines arrive, clients are not available when you need them, and - you know what - life happens.

Your day is a mixed up, convoluted circus and you are the ringmaster who has no choice but to tame the wild lions, swing from the high-wire, and do magic tricks in order to put deals together and or keep them from falling apart. How do you manage to juggle all that at the same time? By being great at multi-tasking, that's how!

Taking the time at the end of each day (personally I like to do this at approx 4:00pm) to review your progress for the day and start preparing a list of priorities for the next day. I cannot stress enough how important it is as a Realtor to keep yourself on track and to take a moment to prioritize those things that must be accomplished.

As you may know, or certainly will discover, on the transactional part of the business there are very few moving parts, although each part is extremely important.

There are components such as deadline dates for conditions, when deposits are due, terms and chattels - the list goes on. But, behind the scenes there is a seemingly long list of items that have to be addressed. Having the ability to launch and maintain a marketing program, advertising, social media presence, self and team education, and keeping up with the ever-changing rules and regulations all takes a good multitasker. Creating lists, prioritizing the tasks, and completing them in a timely manner are true traits of a successful Realtor.

Now if you find that juggling porcupines all day is not your forte, see the next example of another key business building block below.

Delegation

Delegation of duties and responsibilities is essential for you to achieve the goals that you have set for yourself. You truly cannot do everything by yourself and, face it, others just might be better at the task than you are.

Certain personality types tend to want to control every aspect of the business (this is wide-spread in the real estate world); unfortunately, with that type of attitude you can never grow beyond what you only can do personally and that will probably not be enough for you to successfully reach your goals. Having said that, if you are determined to control everything personally in your business, you are destined to do ok, but not great or even remotely come close to your potential.

So many Realtors are afraid to delegate duties and/or let other agents handle certain buyers or sellers. Trust me, if you are running full out, you cannot do a good job with every client you are working with. Let someone help you and you will be pleasantly surprised how they may end up even doing a better job then you could have. My business partner, Glenn Herring, handles a large percentage of our clients.

Not only does Glenn do an excellent job with each and every client that he works with, but I am quite sure that in a lot of cases he did a better job then I might have done.

Delegation gives you leverage, saves you time, and increases the quality of your work as well as reducing your hours and stress. Knowing who to delegate the task to is as important as what you delegate. Don't just hand off jobs and responsibilities for the sake of doing it.

Delegate the right jobs to the right person at the right time. Sound familiar? Yes, it is just like asking the right question of the right person at the right time. Again, look around you and see what person has which skills and then select the best person to handle the task.

Assembling a support group, either on your personal team or by out-sourcing, will allow you to assign and delegate effectively to obtain maximum results. Perhaps you are attempting to create a new marketing flyer and not only do you not have the time to devote to this task, you also have no idea where to start.

In this case, selecting a team member or outsourcing to someone who does possess the skills, time, and the tools to do so, is a perfect example of a task that should be delegated - and delegated to the right person.

People Skills (similar to being a people person)

Not all, but the majority, of top Realtors have excellent People Skills. They are easy and enjoyable to speak to and can hold a conversation on just about any topic with anybody.

We are in the people business and if you find it difficult to engage with other human beings, it might be a personality trait that you will have to work on and improve because it is pretty hard to farm that one out.

I have been fortunate to have traveled to over 40 countries in my life (and counting) and one thing that I have discovered is that a lot of people have either been to the countries I have visited, grew up there, have friends and relatives from there, or want to go and visit there.

Travel, for me, is a terrific icebreaker and I have used it time and time again. Generally, I will pick up on someone's accent or maybe it is something in the house I notice as we tour around upon first arriving.

A couple of years ago, I had recently returned from traveling through Japan and was called to do an evaluation of a home located in my geographical farming area.

Now, I had never met the owner but she considered me to be the neighbourhood expert since she had been receiving my advertising pieces for years. Still, getting the listing was by no means a sure thing.

When I first entered the home, I felt the reception was a bit chilly and I realized that I better act fast to break the ice and build some rapport with the seller. As we walked through the kitchen, I noticed her fridge was covered with fridge magnets, calendars, recipes and other items.

But in the top right corner, all by itself, was a fridge magnet with a picture of a Japanese shrine called Mia Jima, This shrine is located on shores of an island by the same name. Now, as luck would have it, I had just been there the week before, so I asked the seller if she had visited Mia Jima. She had not but her daughter was teaching English in Japan and had just sent that fridge magnet to her. As they say, the rest is history; we bonded over a fridge magnet and once again travel helped me secure yet another listing!

If good conversation or networking skills tend to elude you, then start practicing, for they are essential. Here again, Toastmasters can be a great way to get out of your shell. It is important that you force yourself to regularly attend various events – you can even join a business networking group specifically designed to help you practice meeting new people with different backgrounds and striking up a conversation.

When it comes to improving your People Skills, the more often you put yourself in an uncomfortable situation the better you will be able to handle it. Or, as my friend Rich Robbins likes to say, "Get comfortable with being uncomfortable" Don't just say, "Hey it's not my thing" or "I just wouldn't be comfortable in that situation."

If you are in real estate sales, having People Skills is one of those essentials you constantly should be working on to improve. Too many contacts are made on the golf course, restaurants, and even bars – not to mention conferences and charity group meetings - and you can't afford not to participate.

You have to practice making a connection in the first five minutes of meeting any person. Soon, you will realize that everyone gets nervous meeting people on occasion and it will become second nature. You can do it!

Motivation

The difference between a successful person and others is not a lack of strength or a lack of knowledge, but rather a lack in will.

-Vince Lombardi

Secrets of Success

To motivate an individual, a mass of people or a team of players, can be a daunting task; but to motivate yourself can be one of life's biggest challenges. Real estate sales, by nature, attracts the individualist, the entrepreneur, the person who no longer wants to work for the man, the type of individual that wants to be 100% in control of their future.

They can fire-up the person in the mirror, get him or her dreaming the big dreams, and act on it without having to be pushed and prodded down the path; this is the person that has harnessed the power of Motivation!

The 2009 movie, Invictus, starring Morgan Freeman as Nelson Mandela (the President of South Africa) and Matt Damon (as captain of the South African rugby team), is a perfect example of motivation in many ways. As South Africa hosted the 1995 Rugby World Cup, experts predicted that the South African team would only reach the quarterfinals and no further. The newly elected President Mandela asked the question "How do we inspire ourselves to greatness when nothing else will do and how do we inspire everyone around us?" President Mandela was trying to motivate a country to unite as one nation.

As for the rugby team, they had to change; they had to become greater than they were and they had to become a rugby team that represented an entire nation. Matt Damon had to motivate his team to dig deeper than they have ever dug before, to reach higher than they had ever dreamed of reaching. I will not spoil the movie for you by telling you the out-come, but I strongly suggest, if you need a shot of motivation and a heaping table spoon of inspiration, watch Invictus!

I am the master of my fate; I am the captain of my soul.

-Nelson Mandela

Persistence

When do you give up? When you have had enough, when you are too tired, when you have done more than everyone else around you or more than what you think people think you should have done?

I am not advocating that you pound your head against the wall expecting to get a different result if you just pound it long enough. Taking a different approach, looking at things in a new light or from a different angle may be just what the doctor ordered.

The key thing about being persistent is to decide on a goal and get there by any reasonable means possible. Life's challenges are not a board game with a specific set of rules to go by.

Nowhere is it written that you have to use only one method in life to reach your goals. There is an old saying, "If at first you don't succeed, try, try again." When you are marketing your services to possible clients you have to be persistent and consistent since only Santa Claus gets to work one day each year. Whether you are following up on a for-sale-by-owner or multi-million dollar lead that you have dug up, just asking once for the business will not do; you have to create a battle plan of sorts. Starting with your initial contact, via phone, email or in person, you need to analyze the situation and create a program to follow-up with that lead. It is important to ascertain the preferred communication method for a particular client, but don't be afraid to mix it up a bit. The important thing here is to stay in touch on a regular basis. As a wise Realtor once said, "Last in, first remember!" Learn from this; stay in touch!

Early in my career, I started geographically farming a community where I had successfully sold a lot of new homes. I eventually started sending flyers out to this area in hopes of gaining some additional business. During the first year of sending out flyers and note pads I only had limited success. But I was persistent and continued marketing to the community into the second year; slowly but surely, the phone started to ring and I started listing and selling more and more homes in the area.

One lesson that I have preached for years is that, when it comes to geographical farming of an area, most Realtors give up too early. Do your homework, create and implement a plan, and (most importantly) be consistent and give your plan time to work!

Dream big, set exciting goals, and don't quit until you are happy. Be persistent; it pays off!

When I thought I couldn't go on, I forced myself to keep going. My success is based on persistence, not luck.

-Estee Lauder

Passion

It is said that if you find something you like to do, you will never work again for the rest of your life. Having passion for one's career can make the journey more rewarding and the trip more enjoyable.

I recently spoke to my good friend, Greg Hamre. Greg works with his brother Steve and mother Shirley running one of the top real estate teams in Ottawa, Ontario. Greg not only talks passionately about his real estate career, he has also impressed upon me that his passion for helping people buy and sell their homes is one of the main driving forces behind his tremendous success. People love to listen to someone that is passionate about what they do for a living and enjoy associating and doing business with that person versus the consistent whiner.

The constant whiner is the type of person that, no matter how the market is preforming, they act like Chicken Little with the sky falling on them each and every day. Don't act like Chicken Little; instead, be passionate about your career, for Passion, like Enthusiasm, is truly contagious!

Focus

Welcome to the world of real estate sales, now stay focused!

One of the most important personal traits that you need to possess in our industry is to have the ability to stay focused on the task at hand. Coincidently it is also one of the hardest activities to do in our industry. Now you are thinking "How can I Multi-Task and Focus at the same time?" Well believe it or not, the two can co-exist. You can Focus on Multi-Tasking and you can also Focus on one endeavor at a time. The point is to be present at what you are doing at that time.

I had lunch the other day with 3 of my fellow Realtors and during lunch we made a pact that we would not answer or look at our phones until lunch was over. Not any easy pact to honour and probably for all of us, the longest hour of the week. However we did manage to Focus our attention on the conversation at the table and not be distracted by our phone or someone else's.

Focusing on a client's needs, questions and concerns is a must. In turn taking the time to Focus on your business, planning and just about every other important factor of the business is essential.

Don't be distracted by shiny objects, stay focussed!

These are some of the many personal traits and areas you need to develop in order to stay current, effective and successful in real estate sales.

Top Realtors are constantly improving on their Personal and Professional Development! What are you improving on?

Notes

_____

_____

_____

_____

_____

_____

_____

_____

_____

_____

_____

_____

_____

_____

_____

_____

_____

_____

_____

_____

_____

_____

_____

_____

_____

_____

_____

Notes

Quick Foundation Review

Secret #1

Know enough to know that you don't know!

Whatever topic it may be, accept the fact that you will never be 100% up to-date on the subject. When building the foundation for your business, keep your eyes and ears open; let curiosity dominate and always be willing to learn.

Secret #2

Ask the right question of the right person at the right time!

As your business evolves, new questions will arise that need answers. It is imperative that you continue to ask your questions of the right people at the right time to collect the right answers. You will need this information in order to construct your foundation and to build the rest of your business model.

Secret #3

Adapt and change with the times!

A successful business is a progressive business. Adopting new ideas, revamping old ones, and making sure you stay, maybe not on the cutting edge, but up to-date with the new realities of today's business world. Examine your business structure (your pyramid) on a regular basis to ensure that every level is up to-date.

Secret #4

Take care of everything inside your four walls!

When you examine your business from the ground-up, just as the mighty pyramids were constructed, it is imperative that you make sure that every block and level is solid before you start worrying about someone else's business, other regions, or other country's economies, that have virtually nothing to do with the success of your business. Stay focused on your big picture, not someone else's!

Secret #5

Use your strengths!

Your business should be built on your strengths in order to be successful and sustained in the long run. When you construct that first layer of your business, the foundation, it must be absolutely solid, so it is imperative to ensure your strengths are prominent in the form of key building blocks of your business structure.

Secret #6

Personal and Professional Development!

Will you ever have your business running absolutely perfectly, your foundation as solid as you would like, never have to up-grade or make changes, or be able to take your eyes off the road and let it run on autopilot? Not a chance! Face it; our industry is constantly changing. Heck, in the tech world it seems to change every day, with new inventions (some that will help you, others that will confuse you and be a total waste of time) and socially we develop different expectations, so just accept that things change and so should you.

Overall:

Build and improve upon certain foundational blocks that allow you to exhibit your strengths, while at the same time shoring up the ones that are weaker. Then, it's time to delegate those that you struggle with to someone very capable. As much as you would like to be firing on all cylinders and have constructed a perfect foundation, it probably is not going to happen right off and your foundation will look different than someone else's. The good news is that some blocks can be ignored altogether as long as you are strong enough in other areas to compensate. So, don't kill yourself trying to be everything to all people - including yourself.

Spending the appropriate amount of time evaluating, upgrading and improving the foundation of your business is essential for your success. Make sure you take the time to review, reflect on and revise every level of your business as you go. Businesses always start from the ground up and a real estate sales business is no different.

Remember…basics are not boring…they are essential!

Notes

Notes

Secrets of Success

Secret #7

Industry Knowledge!

Structure of a Real Estate Business

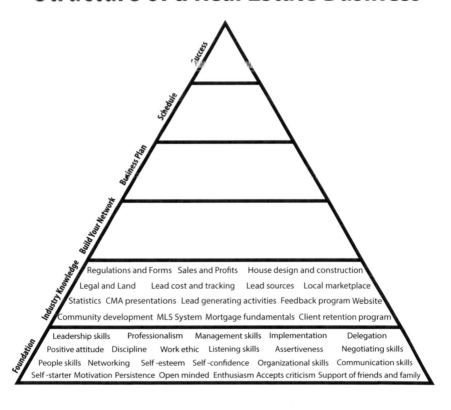

The dumbest people I know are the people that know everything.

-Malcolm Forbes

Acting like you know everything is a sure fire way to fail. Top Realtors never stop educating themselves on their industry.

As discussed in Secret #1 "Know Enough to Know that you Don't Know," is the best strategy to employ.

No matter how much you think you know about a subject, it is better to adopt the attitude of being open minded and curious from day one. Sure, there will be subjects and areas of business that you have experience in, perhaps even in-depth knowledge, but in today's ever changing world, it is better to keep your eye's wide-open and pay attention than to act cocky and strut around with false confidence.

Understanding and keeping abreast of your local market conditions and being aware of the key statistics from sales, average price, turnover rates, absorption rates, inventory levels, and much more will serve you well, but you do not have to become a walking statistic machine; all you need to do is learn to stay up to date with the essential facts.

If you want to gain some quick respect and confidence from your clients, spout off a few key statistics about the local market at the appropriate time and you will be leaps and bounds ahead of your competition, since they will more than likely not be prepared and will have to end up relying on such meaningless descriptive words such as, "Oh, the market is good, not bad or it could be better." Of course we know that will not truly answer the client's questions and, in turn, make you look that much better in the client's eyes.

Then again, not all your competition will be inept, so using and practicing scripts, dialogues, and objection handlers are just a few of many skills you must hone if you hope to win over that precious client. Some Realtors feel that they do not want to use scripts because it may sound like a canned presentation and they would like to come across more real and casual. Big mistake! It is far better to come across as a professional. Professionals are prepared and they practice and improve their skills, so that when they are using scripts, they have internalized them to the point that it sounds real and casual.

As far as objection handlers go, practice them the same as you would practice scripts. You do not want to be stumbling when you hit the first objection, because that may only be the first of many. You should have several objection handlers for each and every common objection that you will run into during the day-to-day operation of your business.

There are times still today when I will get stumped, but fortunately it does not happen too often and there may be times that you will have to wing it. But, with practice and internalization, those times will be few and far between.

When I walk into a home to do a listing presentation, I think of it like I am going on stage for a live performance. I know that I will not be getting a second chance to make a first impression. So it is essential to practice and prepare for those presentations. Next to getting the lead in the first place, it is the next most crucial link in the sales chain.

Park the ego and pride in the back seat and understand that you don't know everything, even if you have been in the industry for 30 years (as a matter of fact, especially if you have been in the industry 30 years!). Things change and I am not just talking technology. As discussed in an earlier chapter, consumer's expectations and wants are changing rapidly and it is imperative that you stay in tune with them.

I suggest prioritizing a list of areas of the real estate industry where you would like to gain knowledge or increase your knowledge (this list will be constantly changing too). The next step is to find courses, books, and seminars that will fill the bill. Your company should have a website with a list of online courses and or recommendations.

If you are at RE/MAX like myself, you can easily log onto RE/MAX Mainstreet at (www.remax.net). From there, you can go to RE/MAX University for a long list of educational programs, tips, forums, downloads, and much more. If you are on the go, as most of us are, you can download the RU (RE/MAX University) mobile app to your smart phone and access it from home, while you travel, sitting at an open house, or from just about anywhere that you can get a Wi-Fi connection.

Your company may have annual or bi-annual conferences that offer great educational sessions or, if you are lucky, speakers may be coming to your market place and presenting on the very subject that you want to focus on. Your local real estate board can also be a tremendous source of information, offering courses, presentations, and sometimes even a help-line to steer you in the right direction. In the previous paragraphs, I have mentioned a short list of areas where more knowledge would be advantageous.

Secrets of Success

I am sure you are aware by now that a full list would be too long for me to create since knowledge in our industry is endless and constantly changing.

So do your homework, talk to top Realtors, and above all, keep your eyes and ears open. There is also a long list of real estate sales training companies that cover the whole gambit; some are focused toward newer Realtors, some are focused toward experienced Realtors, while others specialize in teams. Almost all of them offer a coaching program.

Being coached by a good coach is one of the best things you can do in regard to obtaining education that is tailored to suit you, including your strengths and market conditions. The key word here is good.

I am sad to say that not all coaches that are out there are good ones, so I highly recommend that no matter which training company you select to work with, when they assign you a coach, interview them, be selective, and ask for references.

There are a lot of good training companies out there. As a matter of fact, I really cannot think of a bad one, with most of them focusing on similar programs and systems. Again, you must do your homework and research the top programs; don't just sign up for one because you just sat through a free seminar.

I could make a list of various training companies, but I am not going to play favorites. Instead, ask a few top Realtors you respect for their recommendations, then ask your office manager. In the end, go with what feels comfortable and is within your budget.

Log on to the International Real Estate Mastermind Association www.IREMMA.com. This is an association that I formed in the Fall of 2011, consisting of top Realtors from around the globe who share their best ideas, network, and attend an annual mastermind retreat to expand and share their business knowledge. At these annual retreats we listen to, and are involved in, interactive presentations on current issues. We network and socialize in fabulous locations around the globe. For more information, log on the site above and if you have questions, simply send me an email, as I would be happy to answer them for you.

Knowledge is power.

Knowledge gives you the edge over your competition.

Knowledge gives you control over your future, business, and life.

Increasing your Industry Knowledge will increase your income, guaranteed!

Top Realtors never quit learning! Have you?

Notes

_____
_____
_____
_____
_____
_____
_____
_____
_____
_____
_____
_____
_____
_____
_____
_____
_____
_____
_____
_____
_____
_____
_____
_____
_____
_____

Notes

Secrets of Success

Secret #8

Build your Network!

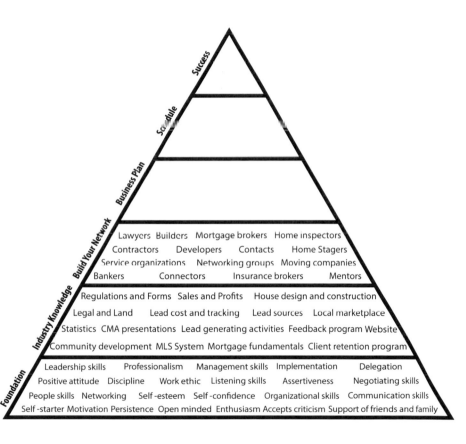

Your network in the real estate world is crucial to your success. You cannot do it all by yourself. A large and strong network magnifies your strengths and leverages your time. It gives you additional assets at your fingertips from trusted sources. This, in turn, will save you time and money.

Secrets of Success

Who you know or, better yet, who knows you, will be one of the catalysts that keep that engine of yours firing on all cylinders, year after year, propelling you to the top. Generally, most real estate agents enter the business from another industry. If you happen to be in the small percentage that came directly from school and into the real estate sales industry, this secret applies to you ten-fold.

Coming from another industry, if it is somewhat related, you might have the extra advantage of being able to leverage some of your contacts or some of your strategic alliances that you have nurtured and built over the years. If you are coming directly from school into real estate, then you will have to virtually start from scratch. But, don't despair; your network can grow quickly and effectively.

Speaking for myself, I did not grow up in my city of Calgary. As a matter of fact, I had only lived in Calgary for a couple of years prior to launching my real estate career, so unfortunately, I did not have a long list of old contacts, past co-workers, and relatives to rely on. All I had was a short list of friends, mostly from the hockey team I was playing for at the time.

I found out quite quickly that if I wanted to survive and succeed in the real estate world, I had to become very proactive, so I started to ask questions of top Realtors in my office and others I would meet during transactions, open houses, and seminars, as to how they built their databases, where they got their clients from and what their top sources of business were.

If I had just sat back and waited for potential clients to call me, I certainly would not have any kind of business and I sure wouldn't be writing a book about success!

Oh sure, we all know those lazy people in our industry. They sleep until noon, spend more time on the golf course than a professional golfer and, to everyone's disbelief, still manage to scratch out a fairly good living, despite their work ethic, or lack thereof.

Well, what are you going to do about it? Are you going to throw your hands up in the air and yell, "That's not fair, how come I don't get all those easy leads?" Well, suck it up buttercup. They are not your leads; they are theirs, so get over it! As we discussed in secret #4, take care of everything inside of your four walls. Don't worry or waste your time being envious of someone else's good fortune. Instead, concentrate and spend your time working effectively on your own business.

Besides, if a Realtor has not had to work hard at generating leads, they will also not cultivate them or do a great job for those clients, so eventually they are going to find it tough to survive on their own should their magic 'lead fairy' disappear. Be happy that you have had to work hard for your own leads, because you know then that you can survive in any market.

The one thing you can do is to get out there and meet people. Make your own connections and build your own network. If you are not currently doing this, then start immediately!

Who do you spend the majority of your time with? Spend is the optimum word here because your time is a currency and should be spent wisely. Who do you hang out or network with on a regular basis? Are they helping you reach your goals or hindering you? Are they building you up or pulling you down? Are they giving you energy or sucking the energy out of you?

It is said that your income is the average income of the five people you spend the majority of your time with. Are you thinking right now that you better get some new friends?

Are you the type of person who makes things happen, or do you just let things happen to you? Are you consciously building your network or are you just settling for whatever comes down the pipe?

I hope it is not the latter, since generally what comes down the pipe is not what you hoped for.

It is time to take charge of your future. Get out there and make those contacts that are going to propel you forward. No more waiting and praying that things will just get better sooner or later because they don't magically get better on their own.

So you never attended an Ivy League school and had the opportunity to build those life-long connections; you were not born with a silver spoon in your mouth and no one is handing you leads left, right and centre. So what? You can easily build your own network, regardless of your starting point in life. Those are just excuses anyway, right?

Let me tell you the story of a friend of mine, Mel Star from Calgary, Alberta. Mel grew up in an area of town called Forest Lawn. No offense to anyone living there, but it can be a tad on the tough side – like, Afghanistan tough.

Like all men, Mel faced many choices in his life, such as where he would live and what he wanted to do for a living. Eventually, he decided to stay in Calgary and get into real estate sales.

Mel told me that he never actually had any other type of full time job since, at the ripe old age of twenty, he starting selling real estate. Mel started from scratch and went out and made the connections that he had to make and built a powerhouse database of contacts. I would have to say that Mel is one of the most connected Realtors in the business with friends, past clients, builders, bankers, and developers.

Mel has surrounded himself with a dedicated team of professionals, all striving to reach team and personal goals. In 2011, Mel's team closed more transactions than any other team in Alberta! As Mel says, "If I can do it, you can do it!"

In order for you to really understand the dynamics of a great network, such as Mel's, I have broken a typical network down into three categories: Contacts, Connectors, and Mentors; you will need all three of these as ingredients to create your formula for success.

Contacts

You will not find a real estate speaker, trainer or coach that does not advocate keeping in contact with your past clients and friends on a very regular basis. These contacts are the life-blood of your business; to ignore them is like burning every bridge you cross.

Far too often, I will run into struggling Realtors and, after a brief discussion, discover that they do not even keep a database, let alone stay in touch with them. This is absolutely inexcusable! Why you would not keep track of, and stay in touch with, people that have trusted you enough to place one of life's biggest transactions in your hands is beyond me.

As you will read in the up-coming secret #9 on business planning, there are simple ways of keeping your name front and centre with your past clients and friends that are not overly expensive and easy to implement.

Your list of contacts can consist of past clients, friends, relatives, past co-workers, service club members from clubs such as Rotary, and Lions. Also, sports teams are an excellent source of business, whether it is baseball, hockey, basketball, or just about any other team sport. Every year, I can count on three of four leads minimum coming directly from my hockey team. The same can be said for my business partner, Glenn's, soccer team. Don't hide the fact that you sell real estate for a living; make sure your fellow players are well aware that you can help them with any and all of their real estate needs. In addition to your sports teams, how about adding the contacts that are created from your children's teams and clubs?

As for service clubs, they are not only terrific organizations helping communities and other needy causes, they can be a great source of business for you. Take the time to get involved, for the rewards are many.

Remember, sooner or later everyone buys and sells real estate. The average homeowner moves every five to seven years.

There have been many surveys completed on this subject, uncovering that the majority of home buyers and sellers when asked, would use the same Realtor. But the majority did not because the Realtor did not stay in touch.

Another group that you absolutely have to add to your database is a group of individuals that I refer to as "Industry Members."

This group of contacts, that is often over-looked, consists of mortgage brokers, lawyers, home inspectors, insurance brokers, and others that are intertwined with the real estate industry. This group has to be built and nurtured over a career to not only be a source of one or two leads, but dozens of leads that in-turn can transform into hundreds of thousands of dollars in commission if handled correctly.

In addition, the relationships that you build with these Industry Members tend to be a two-way street, with you reciprocating business to them as well, professional to professional.

Secrets of Success

Take a break now from reading and make a list of a half a dozen or so contacts in the financial world, builders, developers, trades, or any other real estate industry-related individuals that could be great contacts to help you grow your business:

- _____

- _____

- _____

- _____

- _____

- _____

- _____

How did you make out? Do you have a long list of Industry Members or are you staring at a blank page? Having two or three contacts in each category is the minimum you should have, so if your page is empty start immediately to build this section of your contact database.

Your Industry Member contacts will come and go over the years as certain members will match-up better with certain clients, some will retire or quit, and some will refer more business to you than others. Expect this and make the necessary adjustments as your career progresses along. Joining organizations such as BNI (Business Networking International) addresses this opportunity all in one package. This is a group of business people consisting of one member only from various industries such as: lawyers, mortgage brokers, plumbers, carpet cleaners, insurance brokers, home inspectors, builders, contractors, and practically every industry you can think of.

This group will meet once a week, every other week, or once each month for a breakfast or lunch, gathering to exchange leads and share ideas.

There are many Realtors that enjoy a tremendous amount of business annually from their BNI group. Contact www.BNI.com for more information and to find a local group for you to join.

Staying in touch with your contacts, no matter what category they are in, is an absolute must. Never worry about a little bit of over kill, for that might just waste a little time and money versus not staying in touch on a regular basis which can diminish your business quickly! Staying in touch with your contacts on a regular basis should be built into your business plan/schedule; we will discuss this more in Secrets #9 and #10.

Above all, stay in Contact with your Contacts!

Connectors:

Connectors are the key people in your network. These are the movers and the shakers stretched across your world that are the go-to people, the people that can make your journey to the top easier and faster, not by being lazy, but by being smart. Not having connectors in your back pocket will make your journey unnecessarily harder than it has to be.

We all know these people, the Connectors; they are the ones that know the right people or know the people who know the people that you need to know! If you desperately need a ticket for a sold out concert or a sporting event, these people always seem to find a way to come through for you.

Next time you find yourself at a kitchen party, think, "Who connected me to this party? Was it one person? Was that person responsible for several people in the room showing up?"

As a matter of fact, if you are throwing a party or practically any kind of event, these are the individuals that you want there because where they go, others follow!

Who connected you with your office? Who was responsible for getting you off your butt and out the door to the last seminar, training session or conference? How about your last few transactions? Who was it that connected you to the buyer or seller?

In the real estate world, I do have to say that I am a Connector, for there is not a week that goes by when I do not have a Realtor from my office or scattered offices across the country call or email me and ask me if I know a Realtor in a certain city that they can refer a client to.

I generally ask them if they are looking for a male or female Realtor, younger or older, and any other traits that might match up well with their buyers or sellers, since I know so many Realtors that I want to make sure that I recommend the best Realtor for their client's needs.

How about when you think of your overall advancement in business? Have there been one or two individuals that you have counted on to get you through the closed doors and standing toe to toe with the right people, the decision makers? These unique individuals are the Connectors in your life. They are just like contacts, but on steroids!

You absolutely have to have some of these Connectors in your portfolio because these few individuals can have a powerful impact on helping you to build your business and ultimately a successful career.

Now, think of the movers and shakers in your life, the go-to people or people that know the right people. Who are they? Are there enough of them? Take a few minutes, stand up and stretch, put your thinking cap on, and jot down your list of these super contacts.

It will not be a long list, but it will be very significant list:

- _____

- _____

- _____

- _____

- _____

How did you make out? Did you get two, three, four or five of these Connectors? Is your list too short or is there no list at all? If there are no Connectors on your list, you'd better get cracking and invest some time in this area of your business. These are the golden nuggets that are lying right on top of the ground that can make the difference in growing your business or just surviving in it.

Get Connected to the Connectors!

Mentors

Boy, oh boy! If I could go back in time, there is one thing I would certainly have done more of and that would have been adding more mentors to my life! They would have saved me a lot of time and money; I would not have had to use so much trial and error trying to re-invent the wheel or whatever I was trying to create all by myself.

Mentors can guide you through the maze we call life. They can advise you based on years of experience and collected wisdom that you cannot fathom at your age or at your current level of experience.

So what is a Mentor? Greek mythology describes a Mentor as a father-like figure.

Here is what Wikipedia has to say about Mentors:

"Today's mentor provides expertise to the less experienced individual, helping them to advance their careers, enhance their relationships and build their networks!"

Thank you Wikipedia for backing up my point perfectly.

Building your network is the "Secret of Success" we are focusing on at the moment and Mentors play a significant part in just that.

In your life, you may have already had or still have excellent Mentors. God bless them, for they are the helping hand when times are tough. They steer us around the debris on the road. They are the listening ears that do not judge and then advise us on a course of action best suited for us, whether we like it or not.

Mentors mean well. They are thoughtful, experienced, and willing to offer what they feel is the correct advice for you and your current situation. They tend to serve it up to us in such a manner that, no matter how awful it tastes, we know it is good for us. Besides my parents, of course, I would consider my first mentor in life to be a friend of mine, Bob Kalista. Bob hired me when I was 20 years old to work in a store that he was managing in my hometown. Bob's positive mental attitude was contagious and his outlook on life certainly helped to point me in the right direction.

Our paths took a similar trail, for he entered the real estate world and was one of the influences behind me getting into the industry. Bob and I remain good friends today and our conversations are always positive and optimistic. Thanks, Bob!

Do you currently have Mentors in the key areas of your life helping and guiding you along? Or, are you finding yourself facing into the wind all by yourself with no one readily handy to lean on for support or to point you in the right direction?

Time for you to create yet another list; this time a list of Mentors that are currently in your life. Perhaps you have a family member, co-worker, boss, a coach, or even a speaker or trainer that supports you in this way.

Mentors come in all shapes and sizes; they could be younger or older then you, richer or poorer, as ambitious, or maybe they are very content individuals that feel they have enough in their lives, but are willing to help you grow your business in order for you to obtain what you want and help you fulfill your dreams:

- _____

- _____

- _____

- _____

- _____

- _____

- _____

How did you make out? Do you feel you have enough mentors or are there some gaping holes to be filled? Perhaps you are one of those rare individuals who have surrounded themselves with terrific Mentors in all the crucial areas of life. Or, maybe you are currently staring at yet another blank piece of paper, possibly with some tear stains on it. Think back; are their times in your life that a good Mentor would have certainly made a significant difference?

I know that I definitely could have used a few more Mentors at different times in my life. So don't be shy, too cocky, or too proud to seek out Mentors; they are out there and are waiting to help.

Mentors can be Miracle workers and everyone loves a Miracle!

Stay in Contact with your Contacts!

Connect with the Connectors!

Work Miracles with Mentors!

Top Realtors are always building their networks. What are you building?

Notes

_____

_____

_____

_____

_____

_____

_____

_____

_____

_____

_____

_____

_____

_____

_____

_____

_____

_____

_____

_____

_____

_____

_____

_____

_____

_____

_____

_____

Ken Eddy

Notes

Secret #9

Have a Written Business Plan!

Structure of a Real Estate Business

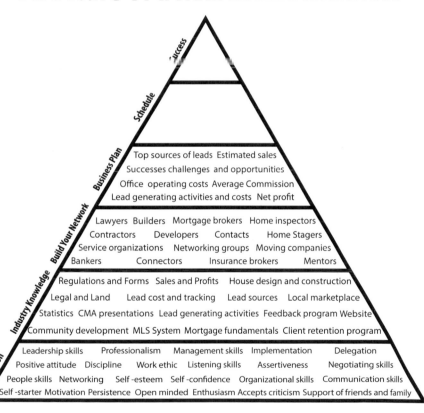

Uh Oh. I can sense the panic setting in at the moment. You are probably saying to yourself, "Business plan… I don't have an MBA or a business degree. How am I supposed to write a business plan? After all, I don't need a business plan to sell real estate. It's easy just sell people's houses and sell houses to people; it's as simple as that!"

Without going back to the previous chapters and regurgitating everything that you have already read, know this: you can sell real estate without a written business plan, but you can sell a heck of a lot more with one!

In the absence of clearly defined goals, we become strangely loyal to performing daily trivia until we become enslaved by it.

-Robert Heinlein

Now, you do not need a business degree or an MBA to write yourself a good business plan. It simply is not that hard if you employ the Secrets that we have already reviewed. After all, Southwest Airlines started with a businessman and a pilot drafting up the original plan for the airlines on a napkin (I wonder if they framed that napkin?!).

Or, you could just sit around the office and wait for a floor duty lead (like that is going to keep you in business for a long time). Yes, maybe someone will walk in or phone the office and you will just happen to get the lead. Then, off you will go and - bang- you sell a house.

Well, even a blind squirrel gets the odd nut! (You do not want to be a blind squirrel; they tend to have a very short life expectancy). And, really, how many times is that truly going to happen to you? Certainly not enough to pay those monthly bills!

Like the vast majority of Realtors, in my early days, I struggled year after year to get the ball rolling. Using credit cards as a necessary bank to fall back on, cutting costs, or doing without was commonplace. I have to admit that it took me years to buy into this Written Business Plan concept, but once I did, what a difference it made to my business! Surprisingly, it is in the actual act of creating your business plan that the true benefit lies. It makes you have a serious look at your current business, what is working for you, what is not working, where your business comes from, and where it is heading. Plus, it shows you the weak areas and the strong areas of your business.

Because I know the Realtor mind-set all too well, I am going to keep this business-planning chapter short, direct, and to the point so it is easy and clear to understand in contrast to how important it actually is.

I know the thought of having a business plan scares the vast majority of Realtors, but don't be afraid. A business plan is easy to construct, for it really only has a few moving parts. But, of course, every part is important.

Here is a breakdown for you of how to create an effective business plan. It consists of five steps (are you still with me? Five steps is nothing):

Step One:

A review of your past year's Successes, Challenges, and Opportunities.

You need to set the time aside to review and plan. This cannot be accomplished on the run. Take the time to collect your data and block off all the time you will need in your calendar to really absorb the information. Have a sober look at last year's results, sales, expenses, and net profit. If necessary, you might have to review the last few years. Be honest with yourself. After all, who are you trying to kid? Some Realtors even go away to a resort or sequester themselves at home to complete this business planning session so as to not to be disturbed. Some take their entire team away to a retreat for the weekend just to be able to focus on their Business Plan and help shape the future.

My business partner, Glenn, and I will set a day that we are going to sit down and review the current year (generally in mid-November of each year) and create our next year's business plan. We both bring with us our views, data, and certainly our opinions on what was good, bad or ugly in regards to the year's performance so far. We review, discuss and create our battle plan for the next year.

Realizing that you can develop a Business Plan that utilizes your strengths, likes, and dislikes as well as one that works with your pocket book is necessary for the survival of your business. If you try to construct a Business Plan that runs contrary to your personality, traits, strengths, and budget, it is doomed to fail. As stated earlier, if you hate doing something, you probably will never be any good at it.

For example, if you cannot stand making cold calls for hours each day, then do not do it! All you will accomplish is to waste endless hours that should be devoted to areas that utilize your strengths. Again, for example, if you are a strong networker and you have no problem striking up a conversation with just about anybody, well then use it to your advantage.

This could be in attending your company's conferences and conventions to network and socialize in order to build referrals from other agents.

During my career, I have had the luxury of reviewing several Business Plans, all of them in different formats. Some were long and complicated and others far too short and weak at best. On the following pages, you will see an actual example of a very simple, but effective, business plan.

It is in a format that I have used for years and will continue to do so. You will find it easy to follow and I truly hope that it helps you in your business.

Sample Business Plan

Your Business Plan
XYZ Real Estate Corp
123 Anywhere Street
Centre City

Table of Contents

Vision and Mission Statement
Previous Year's Successes, Challenges, and Opportunities
Sources of Business, Lead Generating Activities, Marketing Costs, and Gross Profit Estimations
Office Operating Expenses and Estimated Net Profit
Weekly, Monthly, and Yearly Schedules

Vision

Our vision is to create a positive working environment that is not only financially rewarding, but is also one that emphasizes a balanced life between work, time off, and family.

I will dedicate myself to continuing education for the benefit of both my clients and myself.

I will grow my business to be one that is successful in all aspects and pushes the envelope with customer service, one that is respected amongst its peers, achieves our goals, and fulfills our dreams.

Mission

I will give my customers service that is beyond their expectations - service that is complete, precise, and tailored to each of my clients' individual needs and requests.

I will ensure that my transactions are completed in a professional manner with my clients' considerations coming first and foremost.

Secrets of Success

I will have empathy and understanding of the stress and turmoil that the sale of one's home and the purchasing of another one can cause to my clients and will work to ensure that I make their transition as smooth as possible.

I will co-operate with my fellow Realtors and Industry Members in a manner that takes into consideration everyone's concerns and creates a win-win situation.

Previous Year's Successes, Challenges, and Opportunities

Successes

- Achieved sales target of 3 transactions per month
- Reduced flyer costs by hiring a new printer
- Completed mandatory education classes
- Added 56 more people to my database

Challenges

- Lost 12 listings to competitors
- Did not feel I had enough time to work with buyers
- Did not take the time to attend more training seminars
- Needed more listings

Opportunities

- Will be starting a new geographical farming program starting with my own condo complex
- Social Media marketing will be a new focus for me and I will expand my knowledge and create a workable program
- I will hire a buyer's agent to help me out
- I will be taking more courses that focus on listing presentations
- Sources of Business, Lead Generating Activities, Marketing Costs, and Estimated Gross Profit

Past Clients and Friends

	Estimated Costs					
Call two times a year	0					
Meals/ Entertainment	$1,000					
Christmas Card/ Calendar	$1,000					
Other Holiday Cards	$500					
Monthly Newsletters	$2,000					
Buyer possession gift	$1,600					
Notepads	$500					
Email updates to clients	0					
Total	$6,600	20	$7,000	$140,000	$133,400	95%
	Estimated Costs	Estimated Ends	Average Income	Estimated Income	Estimated Profit	Percentage

The above is an example using Past Clients and Friends as one source; below are some suggestions of more sources. You can easily repeat the above process for each one. Of course, the activities and costs will be different.

Additional Sources

- Agent Referrals (other agents referring clients to you)
- Industry Members (mortgage brokers, bankers, lawyers, insurance providers etc.)
- Geographical Farming (areas that you send flyers out to)
- JL and JS (just listed and just sold cards distributed around your listings/sales)
- Website
- Social Networking
- Service Clubs (Rotary, Elks etc)
- Business Networking Groups
- Newspaper/Magazine Advertising
- Duty Leads
- Sign Calls

Estimated Office Operating Expenses and Net Profit

The above is an example of a very simple business plan. I would like to add that Past Clients and Friends are a very profitable source of business, you will find others, such as Geographical Farming, to be very expensive, but almost all sources of business will end up helping you build your very profitable Past Client database.

Estimated Office Expenses	
Office bill	$12,000
Various annual dues	$1,000
Phone	$1,200
Internet services	$300
Stationary and supplies	$500
Real Estate Board	$700
Education and training	$900
Donations	$1,000
Accounting	$1,000
Misc	$500
Total	$19,100

Summary		
Estimated Sales	$140,000	
Minus Estimated Marketing Expenses	-$6,600	
Minus Estimated Office Expenses	-$19,100	
Estimated Net Profit =	**$114,300**	**81%**

All of us start out differently and yet the same. We all could have several sources of business when we first launch our careers, but we generally have one main source that helped us get going. That source could have been your family, friends, past co-workers, or other sources. Mine was new home sales. For two and a half years, I sold new homes in a small subdivision (as well as a few homes to friends). This is what got me through those tough first few years. Like most new Realtors, I did not have much of a plan during those years, but after I resigned from selling new homes to concentrate on resale home sales, a plan started to take shape.

As I have mentioned earlier, my main source of business became Geographical Farming; I sent out flyers, note pads, and fridge magnet calendars to the subdivision where I had just sold dozens of new houses.

I planned out which months I was going to send out a flyer, which months a note pad, and when I was going to send out the fridge magnet calendar.

I calculated the costs and estimated the sales and profit (thankfully there was a profit), but I want to give you a note of caution here: Geographical Farming can be very expensive and can take years to generate a return. I was fortunate because, as I have stated, I sold new homes in the area and my name was well known from day one. Also, since I had created lots of past clients through these sales, I did have a slight advantage over someone just starting from scratch.

Geographical Farming was the basis of my initial plan and then came the creation of a past client retention program to work my database (of course most of my past clients lived in my farm area so they received even more marketing material from me) and I was off to the races.

Over a period of time, my geographical farm grew from 1,700 homes to 4,000 homes, to 8,000 and then eventually to 13,000 homes. My past clients grew from a few dozen to hundreds. Eventually, I added another source of business to my plan and that was Agent Referrals. Over the years, Agent Referrals has become my second largest source of business. I want to thank the many Realtors across the nation that have trusted me with their referrals; please keep them coming. I love Agent Referrals!

I accomplished this by attending several conferences and seminars per year, being a guest speaker, participating on panels, and meeting and staying in touch with Realtors from around the world, just like I would with my past clients.

Business and Business Plans evolve over time. It is impossible for you to write a Business Plan that is as effective five years from now as it will be today. Expect to add to it, change direction, reduce or increase your costs, and other adjustments as your business grows. Do not be afraid to revise it mid-stream; there is no need to throw good money after bad, just ensure that you give your plan a fighting chance. Rome was not built in a day and your business won't be either.

If you are given the opportunity to review someone else's Business Plan, take it!

Secrets of Success

Every so often when I am doing a presentation on Business Planning, I will offer to the audience a copy of my personal Business Plan. All they have to do is just email me. Shockingly, only a handful of Realtors will take me up on that offer.

If they do, it is generally the top Realtors in the room that do and it is usually immediately right from their smart phones.

Are you surprised? I am not; I know why top Realtors would do that and I also know that the bulk of Realtors are sadly complacent and tend to ignore the golden opportunities that are presented to them.

If McDonalds offered Burger King a copy of their Business Plan, do you think that they would take it? You bet your quarter pounder with cheese they would! Again, if you are offered a copy of a top Realtors Business Plan, take it!

Once you have invested the research and dedicated the time to create your own Business Plan - one that is built on your strengths, likes and dislikes and within your budget, your business will grow like it never has before.

You will realize that it is a very significant and integral part of success. You will wonder, in fact, why you had not taken the time to create your Business Plan earlier in your career. If you are new to the real estate industry, then do yourself the biggest favour you can: build your Business Plan!

Great things are not done by impulse, but by a series of small things.

- Vincent Van Gogh

Top Realtors plan for success! What are you planning for?

Ken Eddy

Notes

_____
_____
_____
_____
_____
_____
_____
_____
_____
_____
_____
_____
_____
_____
_____
_____
_____
_____
_____
_____
_____
_____
_____
_____
_____
_____
_____
_____
_____

Notes

Secret #10

Follow a Schedule!

Structure of a Real Estate Business

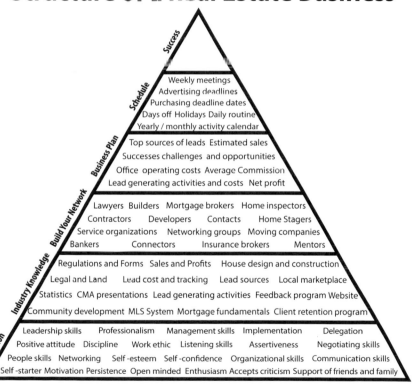

I can hear it now… "I never got into real estate to follow a schedule. I am going to sleep till noon, golf every day, basically come and go as I please." Well, I have a surprise for you. If you do not follow some sort of schedule you will not get very far in this industry.

Remember the saying, "The best part about being in real estate is that you are your own boss, and the worst part about being in real estate is that you are your own boss."

This is when the chickens come home to roost; you need to follow a schedule. If the word "schedule" scares you, then call it a routine, pattern, or whatever you want to call it. But believe me, you have to follow something or you will slowly (or quickly) wither and die on the vine. You need to develop good habits, create productive routines, and be accountable to yourself and others.

Very recently, I was discussing this book with a fellow Realtor and friend from my office, John Mele. John has been in the real estate industry for over 30 years and is consistently one of the top Realtors in our office, year after year.

Here is a quote from John,

Life is a habit; real estate is a habit. Develop good habits.

We all need to be productive, day in and day out, to get and stay at the top of our game.

Develop good habits and control the bad ones!

Having discipline (one of the building blocks in your foundation) is essential to ensure that you accomplish what you set out to achieve. You need to treat your career like a job, so get up and go to work. If you lack discipline, your career in real estate sales will be short lived.

Over the years, I have listened to several speakers proclaim that one of the reasons top Realtors make more money than everyone else is because they work less hours! Time and time again I hear these same speakers preaching that if you work fewer hours, you will make more money. Here is the problem with that: it is not necessarily true. Plus, it is a dangerous rumour to be spreading around. Saying that top Realtors work smarter and very effectively is correct - but not that they hardly work.

I have had the pleasure of interviewing and associating with top Realtors for years and if there is one thing I can guarantee you, it is that they put the hours in. Telling someone that they have to work less hours does nothing but confuse the struggling Realtor and can cause them to take their eye off the ball and question their every move.

You don't get something for nothing and that is definitely true in real estate sales.

You simply cannot work 10 hours per week and expect to maintain a consistent six-figure income.

Real estate sales take commitment and a lot of work in order to be successful at it. Don't be sidetracked by people who want to sell you systems that promote a 20-hour work-week and promise the world.

One summer, not long ago, I had just returned from a three-week holiday to Europe. Upon my arrival home, I called my sister Sharon to see how things were and to let her know that I had returned safely (actually I was not even sure she knew I was traveling). Sharon said to me, "Kenny you are always on vacations." Two things here: My sister is the only one that can call me Kenny and if you want to get under my skin real quick, tell me that I hardly work!

Through gritted teeth, I politely explained to her that the average person gets four months off per year. I let that sink in for a moment and she replied, "Kenny, that is ridiculous" (I love when people take the bait like that). I went on to explain to her that it was simple math: there are 52 weeks in a year, this would mean that there are 104 Saturdays and Sundays, throw in the 10 work days that you would have off if you had a two week vacation and mix in the statutory holidays through-out the year and what do you have? Approx 124 days off, which translates to four months, sister! Taking a three week holiday should not be interpreted as if someone is retired!

And I am not even talking about paid sick days and extra weeks of vacation that someone is generally entitled in a regular job after putting in years of dedicated work.

Top Realtors make more money because they work smart and hard not because they work less! They create a schedule that works for them and their family, they go to work and are productive and, in turn, they can make a very good income. This affords them to go away on more expensive trips and not have to pinch pennies and stay close to home every time they do take a vacation.

Don't be afraid of following a schedule; it is your friend and, in a way, it is your business partner. It puts your plan to work and, in turn, it puts you to work.

Secrets of Success

There are two schedules that I suggest you incorporate into your business:

The first one is a weekly schedule much like you would have at a real job with a real boss for half the money. The second is a monthly schedule, where you would actually insert your business plan.

See the schedules below:

Weekly Schedule

	Monday	Tuesday	Wednesday	Thursday	Friday	Saturday	Sunday
9 A.M.	Office meeting, Lead follow-up	Lead generation and follow-up	Lead generation and follow-up	Lead generation and follow-up	Weekly review Lead generation	Off	Off
10 A.M.	Team Meeting	Toastmasters			Lead follow-up		
11 A.M.	Lead Generation		Deal Follow-up	Deal Follow-up	Deal Follow-up		
12 P.M.	Lunch	Lunch	Lunch	BNI Lunch	Lunch	Lunch	Lunch
1 P.M.	Social Media	Lead Follow-up	Lead Follow-up	Lead Follow-up	Weekend planned for open houses	Appointments	Off
2 P.M.	Lead Follow-up	Appointments Research	Appointments Research	Appointments Research	Appointments Research		
3 P.M.	Deal Follow-up	Deal Follow-up	Networking Coffee	Networking Coffee	Deal Follow-up		
4 P.M.	Day Review	Day Review	Day Review	Day Review	Day Review		
5 P.M.	Dinner	Dinner	Dinner	Dinner	Dinner		
6 P.M.							
7 P.M.	Appointments if necessary	Soccer League	Appointments if necessary	Appointments if necessary	Off		

Of course, everyone will have a slightly different week, with meetings, activities both business and personal that you will want to incorporate.

The next schedule is a monthly/yearly schedule; this is the schedule that you insert your business plan into. As a matter of fact, once you have transcribed your plan into your schedule, you may never pick up your plan for the whole year unless you feel that you have to revise it along the way.

Be sure to schedule in your days off, vacation time, conferences, and seminars. Your schedule will help you take more guilt free time off through-out the year and we all know what happens when you plan a vacation; the work you accomplish prior to taking off is always amazing and, of course, when you return full of energy and drive, your business will grow and so will your profit!

Monthly/Yearly Schedule

January

- 6th Send out flyer to past clients and friends
- 14th to 25th Vacation

February

- 9th Send out flyer to past clients and friends
- 12th to 15th Attend company convention

March

- 6th Send out flyer to past clients and friends
- 12th Send out St Patrick's Day card to past clients and friends

April

- 5th Send out flyer to past clients and friends

May

- 4th Send out flyer to past clients and friends

Secrets of Success

June

- 3rd Send out flyer to past clients and friends
- 12th Send out a summer card to past clients and friends

July

- 8th Send out flyer to past clients and friends
- 15th to 30th Summer Vacation

August

- 5th Send out flyer to past clients and friends

September

- 2nd Send out flyer to past clients and friends

October

- 4th Send out flyer to past clients and friends
- 20th Send out a Halloween card to past clients and friends

November

- 3rd Send out flyer to past clients and friends

December

- 2nd Send out a Christmas card and Calendar to past clients and friends

You can use almost any kind of scheduling tool you like to pull this off. Your iPhone, iPad, BlackBerry, Outlook, or just simply type it into your computer, whatever works for you. I actually put it up on the wall in my office on a large Time Poster. This works great since everyone can view it at a glance. For my day-to-day activities, you may be surprised to hear that I use a paper day timer and large note pad that stay on my desk. Of course, when I am traveling I will enter notes, appointments etc into my smart phone, but I generally insert them into my day timer when I return (hey, it works for me).

Develop good habits, control the bad ones, and spend your time wisely; you only have so much of it!

Top Realtors follow a schedule, not their nose! What do you follow?

Notes

Notes

Success and Your Pot of Gold

Structure of a Real Estate Business

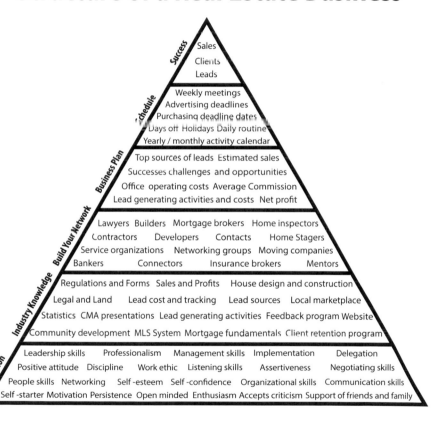

The results of incorporating the ten Secrets of Success into your business model will create a business that generates leads, and lots of them. Of course, after you have obtained these leads, I cannot stress enough the importance of acquiring the skills and working with systems to process and nurture these leads along.

From the generation of the lead to properly listing the house, right through to its eventual sale, it is important to be on top of things and use professionalism from start to finish.

The same can be said for working with buyers; we advise, inform, and assist in the negotiations of a win/win sales scenario.

But remember, you will not sell every house you list or successfully sell a home to every buyer you work with. Real estate, like a lot of sales industries, is a numbers game. The creation of leads, and lots of them, is a must. In order to do this successfully, you need to focus on your business structure and ensure that you have incorporated the ten Secrets of Success that you have just read!

These ten Secrets of Success are only the beginning, the platform and structure that your business is built on. The more attention, time, and effort that you give in implementing the ten Secrets, the greater your success and the bigger your pot of gold.

Review the Ten Secrets of Success

1. Know enough to Know that you Don't Know!

Are you prepared and willing to:

- Acknowledge that you may not have been born with all the answers?
- Open your mind to new ideas, quit using excuses and believing in myths?
- Jump right in and start, instead of waiting until everything is perfect?
- Take charge of your own education?

2. Ask the Right Question of Right Person at the Right Time!

Are you prepared and willing to:

- Search out the answers to your questions?
- Write down and organize your questions?
- Seek out the right person to answer your questions?
- Ask those questions at the right time?
- Listen to and take action with the answers?

3. Adapt and Change with the Times!

Are you prepared and willing to:

- Get, and stay, up to-date with the changes to our industry?
- Market yourself and your inventory with modern techniques?
- Meet your client's expectations?
- Operate your business on a current and effective platform?

4. Take Care of Everything Inside your Four Walls!

Are you prepared and willing to:

- Control your business and not worry about someone else's?
- Ignore problems that are outside of your control?
- Make sure that your business is running at 100%?
- Listen to advice from only people who are qualified to give it?

5. Use your Strengths!

Are you prepared and willing to:

- Search out and recognize your strengths?
- Focus on your strengths?
- Implement your strengths?
- Practice your strengths?

6. Personal and Professional Development!

Are you prepared and willing to:

- Develop your personal traits and characteristics?
- Focus on the basic building blocks, these should be the key elements of your business?
- Repair the weak areas or delegate them?

7. Industry Knowledge!

Are you prepared and willing to:

- Adopt an attitude of curiosity?
- Improve your knowledge of our industry?
- Take advantage of the many education options that are available to you?
- Practice your skills?

8. Build your Network!

Are you prepared and willing to:

- Create and expand your network?
- Build contacts in the key areas of the industry?
- Develop relationships with the connectors in your life?
- Seek out mentors for their support and advice?

9. Have a Written Business Plan!

Are you prepared and willing to:

- Buy into the fact that you need a business plan?
- Create a plan based on your strengths, likes and dislikes and within your budget?
- Review your successes and challenges while recognizing the opportunities?
- Implement and follow your plan?
- Reflect, review and revise accordingly?

10. Follow a Schedule!

Are you prepared and willing to:

- Design a schedule that helps to implement your plan?
- Schedule in your personal and family time as well as your business requirements?
- Have the discipline to stick to your schedule?
- Develop good productive habits and routines?

Well, there you have it, ten "Secrets of Success." These are ten key aspects and characteristics of top Realtors. I do not call these secrets basics, I call them essentials and they are critical to your success!

You now have two choices: you can disagree with these Secrets of Success and continue running your business the same way you have been, getting the same results year after year. Or, you can incorporate these Secrets of Success into your business, recognizing the weak or missing building blocks and taking the appropriate action to rectify the problems.

If you are brand new to the real estate sales industry, you have the advantage of having read what has taken me 25 years of experience selling real estate to learn and understand. I encourage you to take advantage of what you have just read and incorporate these Secrets of Success into your new career immediately.

Have a look at the top Realtors in your office/company and then have a look at the struggling Realtors. Think about what they say and evaluate what they do, then come to your own conclusions.

If you are a seasoned Realtor, but feel that you have not obtained the success that you desire, don't hesitate to make the adjustments needed to get you where you want to go. Some of these secrets you may already be aware of and others you may have overlooked.

Either way, take advantage of them and use them to your benefit. I know that sometimes to admit that we may not have been doing things properly (perhaps for years) and maybe not keeping up with the changes in our industry is tough, but we all have to put pride and ego to the side and move forward - for your sake and for your family.

As I stated right at the start of this book, I don't pretend to have all the answers, but I have some of them and they are the ten Secrets of Success that I have just laid out for you. Ten reasons why 10% of Realtors control 90% of the business. I hope you use them; I hope your business and life improves because of them.

Carpe Diem, "Seize the Day"- this is your business, your life, and your future. Take charge of it and go put these Secrets of Success to work for you today!

I will leave you with a few words that I believe capture the essence of the Secrets of Success:

Words of Wisdom

Watch your thoughts, they become your words.

Watch your words, they become your actions.

Watch your actions, they become your habits.

Watch your habits, they become your character.

Watch your character, for it becomes your destiny.

- Author Unknown

Ken Eddy

About the Author

Ken Eddy started his Real Estate sales career more than 25 years ago. He currently runs one of the top real estate teams in Western Canada. Ken works out of RE/MAX Real Estate Central in Calgary, Alberta, Canada, which continues to be the world's busiest RE/MAX office (based on actual closed transactions) consistently year after year.

Ken excels at sharing his knowledge of what it takes to be successful in today's real estate sales world. Since 2004 he has hosted dozens of seminars across the country in addition to his annual Mastermind Retreat. This retreat brings like-minded Realtors together to share and exchange ideas and systems for everyone's benefit. Ken is the father of two grown children, Paul and Sarah. He has traveled to more than 40 countries including backpacking through Thailand, Japan, Cuba, Spain, Croatia and Italy. He has also toured and played hockey in Russia, Sweden, Germany, Poland, Czech Republic, Hungary and several other countries.

Ken believes in working smart and hard in order to live a balanced lifestyle that is achievable by any Realtor if they are willing to learn, apply and work hard – no matter the current economy. Ken has been featured and recognized at numerous RE/MAX conferences. He is an International speaker having presented in many cities across Canada and the U.S.

For more information on Ken's retreats and seminars, and to book Ken to speak at your next event, visit Ken's seminar website:

www.keneddyseminars.com